MW01065756

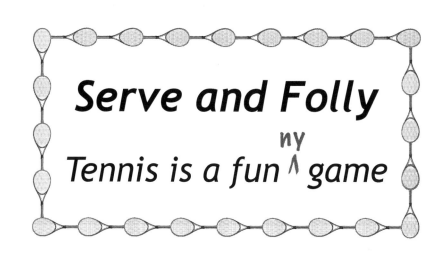

Serve and Folly

Tennis is a fun^ny^ game

Written by
Howard Elgison

Illustrated by
Jim "Catfish" Brown

Cover Design by
Eileen Easler

Publisher:
Sweetwater Oaks Publishing Company, LLC
907 Woodcraft Drive
Apopka, FL 32712

Copyright © 2013 by Howard Elgison
Illustrations Copyright © 2013 by Jim "Catfish" Brown

Library of Congress Control Number: 2013935311
ISBN Number: 978-0-615-78486-1

First Edition: April 2013

Book layout by Eileen Easler:
E2 Exhibits & Displays, Inc.
1925 High Meadow St.
Johns Island, SC 29455

Website:
www.serveandfolly.com

E-mail
publisher@serveandfolly.com

To Denny, my first tennis buddy
Rally In Peace

Acknowledgments

I'd like to thank the following people:

My wife, Susan, who was a constant source of inspiration with such words as, "If you don't finish this book you have to re-grout the bathroom."

My tennis friends, who provided equally inspiring messages like, "Would you just get the damn thing done. We're sick of hearing about it."

My friend and artist Jim "Catfish" Brown for his illustrious illustrations.

Editor Beth Bruno. I kept trying to sneak mistakes and typos past her, but she kept finding them. In addition, Beth made numerous suggestions that improved the manuscript.

Layout artist Eileen Easler for turning a hodgepodge of text, titles and illustrations into a finished product, and for creating such an eye-catching cover.

Barbara Delahoussaye for the back cover picture of the dude with the super-sized racket.

Ron and Pat Peterson for use of said racket (which, by the way, is a comedic prop, not a compensation device).

Lin Lewis for the final proofreading.

All the people responsible for inventing personal computers, the Internet and word processing software, especially the cut/copy/paste function.

Howard Elgison
March 2013

Introduction

There's really no need for an introduction to this book. The title, subtitle and cover tell you all you need to know about it. So to keep this introduction from being a total waste, here are a few jokes.

A little girl comes home after her first day of kindergarten and her mother asks, "How did you like school?"

"It was a waste of time," says the girl.

"Why?" asks her mom.

"I can't read, I can't write and they won't let me talk."

An 85-year-old Jewish man walks into a confessional and says to the priest, "Father, yesterday was my 60th wedding anniversary and I celebrated by hiring two young ladies of the evening for an all-nighter."

The priest gasps and says, "That's a terrible sin. How long has it been since your last confession?"

"I'm Jewish," says the man, "I've never been to confession."

"So why are you telling me?" asks the priest.

"I'm telling everybody," he replies.

Several years ago, our family was vacationing in England during the month of October. We took our rackets, and, on one glorious day, we were able to play in London's Hyde Park Tennis Centre in shorts and short sleeves.

As we left the court I said to one of the locals, "Nice day, isn't it?"

"Nice?" he said. "This is the best weather we've had in 600 years."

Actually, there is one useful piece of information to convey. At the end of each chapter there is a quote page, using both players and commentators as the source. Some are intentionally amusing, others inadvertently so.

The Pronoun Predicament

In writing a book about sports, one often alludes to a generic "player," which inevitably requires pronouns that reference said player. Grammatically speaking, it is acceptable to use the masculine forms "he" and "him" to cover both genders. While it might be correct it doesn't seem equitable, given that roughly half of all tennis players are women.

It's a problem for which there are no satisfactory solutions. If one uses only male forms, one is being exclusionary, even sexist. If one uses only female forms, one is pandering to political correctness, or, worse yet, being a wuss. If one uses gender-neutral plural forms "they" and "them," which are grammatically questionable for a singular antecedent (or downright wrong according to some pronoun mavens), one is being a cop-out.

So one may as well go for the cycle—sexist, wuss and cop-out—by using all three options. The rationale is based on the inverse of the maxim, "If you try to please everyone you please no one," which is, "If you try to please no one you please everyone." (Hopefully.)

Acronyms

Tennis

WTA (Women's Tennis Association)
Established in 1973, the WTA is the principal controlling body for the women's professional tour and the player ranking system.

ATP (Association of Tennis Professionals)
Established in 1972, the ATP is the principal controlling body for the men's high-level professional tournaments and the player ranking system.

ITF (International Tennis Federation)
Established in 1913, the ITF is the controlling body for the Grand Slam tournaments as well as international competition such as the Davis Cup and Fed Cup.

USTA (United States Tennis Association)
Established in 1881, the USTA is the national governing body for tennis in the US.

Non-Tennis

BTW (By the way)

IMO (In my opinion)

FWIW (For what it's worth)

OTOH (On the other hand)

EAWTA (Enough already with the acronyms)

To play Good Tennis, what divine joy
Can fill our leisure or our minds employ
Let others play at other things
The King of Games is the Game of Kings
J.K. Stephen

"The depressing thing about tennis is that no matter how good
I get, I'll never be as good as a wall."
Comedian Mitch Hedberg

"The last one."
Ivan Lendl, on being asked what he considered to be the most
important point in a match

Table of Contents

Prologue 1

Chapter I... 3
It's a Simple Game

Chapter II 25
Take Two

Chapter III 41
Musings from No-Man's Land

Chapter IV 75
Pros and Cons

Chapter V 99
Court Jesters

Chapter VI 117
The Ten Commandments of Tennis

Chapter VII 123
The Senior Game

Chapter VIII... 133
A Brief History of the Game

Chapter IX 149
The Last Shot

Prologue
A Personal Tennis Journey

When I graduated from college and joined a world that doesn't give partial credit for being close, I decided to find a sport that reflected my new reality. I tried both running and triathlons, but neither was much fun for me.

Then one day I passed by the local college tennis courts and stopped to watch the matches. As I saw those guys and gals race around the courts, displaying an impressive combination of skill, athleticism and competitiveness, I said to myself, "That's for me!"

So I bought a racket and some balls and set out on what would become a lifelong adventure. Initially, it was a pretty frustrating endeavor, but as I gradually improved I began enjoying the game more and more.

After about a year I was hooked. Hooked? Hell, I was obsessed. All I could think about was playing tennis. Oh, I still went to work and still fulfilled my conjugal obligations, although not on the night before a big match, but my heart was always on a tennis court.

Finally, my wife decided she'd had enough. "Your tennis fixation is disrupting our family life," she said. "You need professional counseling."

Reluctantly, I agreed and made an appointment with a psychologist. On the day of the appointment I walked into her office and we exchanged introductions. Then we sat down and she asked, "What's troubling you?"

"Well, doc," I replied, "tennis has taken over my life. All I can think about is playing."

"Me too," she said. "Let's go hit some."

So we did, and I haven't stopped since.

Brain Surgery
(It's not exactly tennis, but it's still pretty tricky.)

Chapter I

It's a Simple Game
(No, it's not)

In theory at least, tennis is a simple game that can be broken down into four basic steps:

1) You hit a ball back and forth over a net
2) You miss
3) You scream at yourself for being a worthless hack
4) You start over

It's certainly not as difficult as, say, brain surgery, which probably requires nine or ten steps. Then again maybe it is, because I have witnessed an eminent neurosurgeon have a full-blown meltdown on a tennis court, complete with cursing and racket-throwing. It's doubtful he acts that way in the operating room, even when things are going badly. (Although it would be kind of funny to hear a surgeon scream self-abusive epithets such as, "You idiot! Keep your eyes on the artery!" Or, "Get your scalpel back quicker, you dolt!" Well, maybe not so funny to the patient.)

I think anyone who has played tennis for an extended period would agree that it takes a great deal of time and effort just to attain a respectable level of skill. Of course, you can shorten the learning curve by taking lessons from a qualified pro. Or you can read a book like this one, but I doubt it will help you. In the many years that I've been playing this game I've learned a great deal about it and it hasn't helped me very much. It turns out that there is a vast difference between knowing how to play good tennis and actually playing good tennis.

However, if you take nothing useful away from this book, there is one thing that is absolutely guaranteed to help you play better. You've heard it a million times so once more won't hurt. Ready? Drum roll please…

KEEP YOUR EYES ON THE BALL!

When instructors say, "Keep your eyes on the ball," they mean focus, follow, gape, gawk, gaze, glimpse, glare, inspect, leer, look, observe, ogle, notice, peer, peek, peep, perceive, scan, scope, scrutinize, see, sight, spy, stare, view, watch and witness it. (So many ways to do it yet so hard to do.)

Watching the ball is by far the most important thing to remember on a tennis court. Everything else is just eyewash. (That's not true, of course, but it makes for a good one-liner.) There's just one drawback. The better you watch the ball the better you'll hit it, but the less time you'll have to admire your shot, which is one of the best parts of the game. Ironic, isn't it?

So much for that, let's move on to…

Stroke Production
The First Serve

For many people, the serve is the most frustrating of all the strokes. However, it really shouldn't be because it's the one stroke over which you have complete control. You simply toss the ball where you want it to be when you hit it. (Unless you're one of those dweebs who tosses the ball all over the place and has to catch every third one. That's very annoying, so stop it.)

Here's the typical serving scenario. You start a match and, right from the get-go, your first serve is working great. You're hitting it accurately, consistently and with good pace. You think to yourself, *Oh man, I've got it now. If I can just keep the same grip, motion and toss, I'll never have to worry about my first serve again.* Seriously? Haven't you been down this road before (haven't we all?) and has it ever worked out that way? In fact, the very next day your serve could be all over the place, and you can barely find the service box much less hit the corners. So what is going on? How can your serve be so good one day and so bad the next?

Fortunately, modern sports science has the answer. It is a combination of physiology, kinesiology and mental awareness that will have you serving great for the rest of your life. Unfortunately, I have no idea what the answer is, but if you find out please let the rest of us know. There is another caveat to the service situation. Any improvement you make to your first serve lasts for only one match.

The Second Serve

Here's a mantra we all say, if only subconsciously.

I am a good person.

I am a pretty good tennis player.

I am better than my second serve.

While the first two statements might be true, the third one is not. If you have a lame second serve skilled players will eat it up. If you are playing with people who don't, then they aren't very good and when you step up a level you're in for a nasty surprise.

Serving in tennis is like making love. Anyone can do it well the first time; the second time takes a lot of work. Except that in tennis if your first serve is in, you don't have to do it again, so this isn't a very good analogy. But you should still practice your second serve.

The Service Return
It's all about where you stand

Obviously, the service return is not a single stroke or even an assortment of strokes. Rather, it is an embodiment of the wide-ranging personalities and attitudes of tennis players. For example, if you're the impetuous, progressive type who seeks immediate results and rapid changes, you'll stand right at the baseline or even inside it. From this aggressive position you can hit outright winners and forcing shots, particularly when you're in the left court. Unfortunately, you will tend to make numerous errors, some of which could be very costly.

OTOH, if you're the cautious, conservative type who is hesitant to adopt radical ideas without serious deliberation, you'll stand well behind the baseline and give yourself more time for the return. From this defensive position you can get a high percentage of balls in play, but you will miss opportunities to take the offensive, even though you're convinced your position is correct. Plus, you feel much more comfortable in the right court.

If you're in the final category, the independents (a.k.a., indies), you will see both the positive and the negative attributes of the others. Depending on the situation, you might join the progressives at the baseline or stand with the conservatives well behind it. Quite often, however, you'll feel more comfortable in a location midway between the two extremes.

Although the progressives and conservatives command the spotlight with their constant bickering about whose receiving philosophy is superior, it is usually the indies who determine the outcome of matches. Furthermore, the indies, unlike the progressives and conservatives, do not try to impose their return position on others, believing that all players should decide for themselves where to stand.

The Forehand

It's a forehand, for cryin' out loud. Just take the racket back and whack the ball. Anyone can do it. (In tennis instruction terms that's known as the Occam's Razor method.)

The One-handed Backhand

The problem with most people's one-handed backhands is they watch too much television. Specifically, they watch too many pros on television hitting smooth, flowing topspin backhands, even off their opponents' first serves, and they think, *Heck, that looks easy.*

And it is if you've spent a good part of your life working on it, being coached on it and having the natural talent for it. Otherwise, stick with the slice. It might not get you on the Tennis Channel's highlight reel, but it will give your opponents a lot more chances to miss their topspin backhands.

The Two-handed Backhand

When people ask me, "If you could go back in time and change one thing about your life, what would it be?" my answer is always the same. I would learn a two-handed backhand right from the start. To tennis players this makes perfect sense, but when non-tennis people hear that kind of response they are always taken aback and invariably ask follow-up questions such as, "That's it? Couldn't you strive for a loftier goal, like world peace?"

I explain to them that given the choice between working for world peace or developing a killer backhand, most tennis players would, with very little reflection, choose the backhand. It's not that tennis players are *against* world peace. We just don't see how it's going to improve our games, so it's not very high on our priority lists.

After trying unsuccessfully to hit a two-hander for over a year I finally concluded that my non-dominant hand is useful only for service-tossing and beer-holding. So I envy those who can hit this shot well. Not only do they have a potent weapon in their tennis arsenals but, over their lifetimes, they'll spill a lot less beer.

The Volley

The secret of volleying is like the secret of happiness. Most of us believe such a thing exists; we just don't know what it is.

It really shouldn't be that way because the volley is such a simple stroke. At least it is when you're standing at the net during the warm-up and someone is hitting medium-paced balls into your wheelhouse. However, in the heat of a match, when you have to make very quick adjustments while you're moving, it's not so easy. Personally, I think volleying is more of an innate skill than a learned one. So, IMO, the secret of good volleying is to be born a good volleyer.

As for the secret of happiness, this could be one of those "be careful what you wish for" situations. What if you discovered the secret of happiness, and it didn't make you happy? Now that would be depressing.

The Swinging Topspin Volley

Hitting a swinging topspin volley is like eating a foot-long chili cheese dog. You know you're going to regret it afterwards, but you just have to go for it once in a while. However, you have the same inherent danger in both cases. If you happen to feel good after eating your first chili dog, you'll be tempted to eat a few more. Similarly, if you happen to hit a winner with your first swinging volley, you'll be tempted to go for more.

This is a huge mistake because, just as consuming multiple chili dogs will end your evening in a hurry, hitting a lot of swingers will end your match in a hurry. Of course, if you're running late and have to get off the court quickly you should go for as many swinging volleys as you can. In no time at all you'll be headed for your house or, in the case of the chili dogs, for your outhouse.

The Overhead

Think of the overhead as a serve with an extremely high toss. Of course, that just puts you in the same situation you have with your serve so it's really not much help.

Here's another approach. Say you mis-hit way too many overheads. Okay, let's review your technique.

1) You get into position quickly by taking small adjusting steps. *Check*

2) You rotate your body such that you're sideways to the ball. *Check*

3) You get your racket into the hitting position. *Check*

4) You point your non-racket hand at the ball. *Check*

5) You watch the ball *almost* to the point of impact. *Check*

That's the way I do it, so I don't see the problem. Maybe you should have your local pro take a look.

The Backhand Overhead

There's a reason why this is called "the toughest shot in tennis." There's also a reason why, when pros teach this shot to club players, they have the players sign waivers releasing the pros from responsibility in the event of death, dismemberment or double hernia.

The Lob

I once saw a bumper sticker that read, "Real men don't lob." And I remember thinking, *Yeah, well, real men don't win many matches either.* A more appropriate slogan would be, "When in doubt, lob."

Like a faithful old dog that has been in your family for years, the lob is your loyal and trusted companion. When your forehand fails, your backhand bails and your service sails, the lob will be there for you. Like the devoted old dog, the lob will ask very little of you. Just stroke it once in a while so it knows you care.

"And how does one hit an effective lob?" you ask. You're kidding, right? Of course, you are. That's the beauty of the lob. Anyone can hit it, anytime and from anywhere on the court.

If you disdain the lob when you're young, you will regret it as you get older because you will need it more and more. You should treat the lob with the respect it deserves, just like your beloved dog. Some days they're the only friends you have.

The Topspin Lob

This is one arrow that's best left in the quiver, most of the time anyway. I usually pull it out when I'm comfortably ahead, say by a score of 5-2, 40-love, because 5-2, 40-15 is still a pretty safe lead.

The Drop Shot

First, a few questions to see if you're cut out for the drop shot.

1) Do you have a family history of sadism?

2) Do you enjoy making opponents frantically scramble around the court, possibly inducing a cardiac event?

3) Do you get a thrill out of inflicting mental anguish and bodily injury?

If you answered "yes" to at least two of these questions then this is the shot for you. Technically, there's really not much to the drop shot. All you need is a soft touch and a callous disregard for human life.

(Here's a helpful hint to opponents of drop shotters. Do not let them supply the balls. They will invariably bring the extra-duty ones, especially when playing on a clay court. Heck, they'd use the ten-and-under nerf balls if they could.)

The Sharply-angled, Half-volley, Drop Shot

The reason some people try such ridiculous shots is that they are under the spell of a logical fallacy known as "confirmation bias." That is, they preferentially remember the one out of three times they make the shot, mainly because it's so impressive when it works, and conveniently overlook the two out of three times they misfire.

If their opponents are smart, they will cheer enthusiastically when someone makes a shot like that with comments such as, "Wow! Great shot! Just like the pros!" Naturally, this encourages players to keep going for it, missing two for every one they make.

The above is a standard tennis ploy. You entice your opponents into trying high-risk shots by showering them with praise on the rare occasions when they make one. Meanwhile, you concentrate on winning the majority of the routine points and, quite likely, the match.

The Ultimate Tennis Tragedy

Before moving on to tennis strategy, there is one more subject involving stroke production that must be broached. But be warned, it can be very painful.

Here is the situation…

Your opponent has hit a routine shot to your forehand side, not very deep or hard. You quickly run over to cover the ball and get yourself in just the right position. You get your racket back early and you watch the ball intently. You swing smoothly and evenly, shifting your weight to your front foot just as your tennis pro taught you, and, CLUNK, you hit the ball way off center and into the bottom of the net.

You've done everything correctly and still butchered the shot. If this happens regularly it is the ultimate tennis tragedy because there is only one conclusion that can be drawn: You're not very good at this game and you probably never will be.

Oh, your tennis friends can offer you hollow words of encouragement such as, "Just keep at it, you'll get better." (No, you won't.) Or, "Everyone has a bad day." (Sure, but not every day.) Or, "At least you won't have to restring your rackets very often since you hit most of your shots off the frame." (Now that's true, but it's not very consoling.)

Your friends might also propagate the Great Tennis Lie by saying, "Don't worry about it. You're getting good exercise, you're playing with your friends so just enjoy yourself. It doesn't matter how you play." Like hell it doesn't. No matter what your level, if you play lousy you're going to be miserable, and if you play lousy all the time, you'll be frustrated, angry and depressed.

Pretty soon it will adversely affect the rest of your life. Your relationships will begin to disintegrate and you will cease performing personal hygiene functions. You will end up living in a hovel with gingivitis (you, not the hovel) having collected way too many hamsters, and, for some odd reason, a goat. If I've seen it once I've seen it a thousand times.

If the above describes you, then perhaps it's time to rethink your choice of sports and switch to bowling, or better yet, golf. Now golf has some wonderful features. You get to ride in a cart and you can drink while you play. In fact, some golfers get better when they drink. Also, the ball isn't moving when you hit it and your opponents can't directly affect your shots. How hard could it possibly be?

On to the next subject which is…

Strategy
Singles

There are few tennis topics more overrated than strategy. This is especially true in singles because your game is determined by the shots you *can* hit, not by the shots you *should* hit. Furthermore, to a large extent, your opponent's strengths and weaknesses dictate your strategy.

Here are some examples.

Situation: Your opponent has a weak backhand
Strategy: Hit to his backhand

Situation: Your opponent doesn't move well
Strategy: Make her move

Situation: Your opponent can't handle 130 mph serves
Strategy: Hit 130 mph serves

You get the idea.

Doubles

Doubles is a different story because with two people on a side and numerous rapid-fire points, court positioning becomes paramount. The basic idea is to put your team in the best situation, offensively and defensively, to return your opponents' most likely shots. However, if you've ever participated in a club-level doubles clinic, you know this rarely happens.

For example, the teaching pro will diagram an ideal doubles point as follows.

1) The server hits a first delivery directly at the receiver who hits a medium-paced return.

2) The net-man poaches, hits a crisp volley down the middle and continues to the other side of the court.

3) The server, seeing his net-man move, covers the vacant half of the court.

4) The receiving player hits a lob to the server's side.

5) The server, being in the right position, hits an overhead deep down the middle.

6) The net-man, anticipating a weak return, steps toward the center of the court, very close to the net and smacks away the volley.

However, this is what actually happens.

1) The server hits a first delivery directly at the receiver who hits a medium-paced return.

2) The net-man poaches but doesn't move forward so he catches the ball below the net and pops up the volley. In addition, he stops in the middle to watch his shot.

3) The server, not knowing what his partner is doing, gets caught in no-man's land.

4) The receiving player hits a groundstroke at the server's feet.

5) The server hits back a weak, floating shot.

6) The receiving player takes a wild swing and whacks the ball into the bottom of the net.

7) The serving team slaps a high-five as the pro does a face-palm while thinking, *and people wonder why I drink.*

So much for strokes and strategy. Let's get to the really important parts of the game, the parts that are sadly overlooked by the pros and instruction books.

The Let Game

The Let Game, and, no, it's not a misprint, is defined as "Any ploy, ruse or deception you use to get another first serve." Senior players are especially adept at this, particularly those with hearing problems. They come to the court without their hearing aids and when someone calls the ball "out" they either don't hear it or pretend they don't hear it. They charge the net like deranged water buffalos and, when they see that play has been stopped, they look totally befuddled. When someone says that the ball was called out, they respond with, "Huh?" Invariably, they are awarded another first serve.

The next ploy is the fence-clearing routine. Here's how it works. If you miss your first serve and your opponent hits it back, you let the ball go all the way to the fence no matter how close it comes to you. Then you make a big production out of walking over to the fence and "clearing" the ball even if it's only half an inch from the fence. You do this very slowly to ensure yourself of that "take two" call we all love to hear.

The next is a male ploy and involves the appearance of a female anywhere near your court. It goes like this. You've missed your first serve but you spot a woman either walking towards your court or sitting nearby. Being a typical male you have to check her out, maybe even wave to her, which will generally cause your opponents to glance in her direction. As soon as they do that you say, "Are you guys here to play tennis or look at women?" They shake their heads, knowing they've been suckered, and give you two serves.

The final one is a female ploy and starts off the same as the male ploy with a missed first serve and a woman approaching or sitting nearby. From here the plot changes. You stop before your second serve and give her an admiring look. When your opponents glare at you reproachfully, without the offer of a first serve, you say, "I'm so sorry, but she is wearing the cutest outfit." Not to be sexist, but most women are going to look, and, once they do, it's "take two" time.

A few words of caution here. These powerful techniques are not to be used frivolously and should be implemented only at crucial times of a match. If you overdo them, your opponents won't give you another first serve even if a meteorite slams into your head. Also, be advised that cheap theatrics such as bouncing a ball off your foot, having a phony coughing spell or swatting at non-existent bees won't work. We've all seen these tricks, a lot of us have tried them, so don't even bother.

The Art of the Line Call

This is a seriously neglected part of the game because most people simply call balls "in" or "out," but there is much more to it than that. However, before going into the details let's get one thing straight. If you're not 100% certain that a ball is out, then it's in. Ultimately, we rely on our opponents to make honest line calls. If we can't do that, then all hope for maintaining a civilized society is lost. Maybe that's going a little overboard, but it's pretty bad when you can't trust your opponent's integrity.

Here are some examples of creative line-calling…

1) The phony sympathy call. "Gosh, that was close. I just hate to call it out."

2) The buildup to a letdown call. "Great shot… too bad it was long."

3) The sarcastic call. "Your shot was fine, the court was too short."

4) The insulting call. "Were you aiming for *this* court?"

There are times when people will question a call, usually with a simple, "Are you sure it was out?" For this situation you need some snappy responses.

"Out? That ball wasn't even in the right zip code."

"I'm sure it wasn't in. The only other choice is out."

Another effective gambit is when you're playing doubles on a clay court and your opponent hits a shot very close to the baseline on an important point. When you check the mark you see that it was just out, but you slump your shoulders and hang your head, intimating that the ball was good. Your opponents will be thrilled until you say, "That was long."

Chances are at least one of your opponents will take this badly and spend the next few games trying to cream you with the ball. Of course, most of his shots will be errors.

Many people would consider this kind of line-calling to be gamesmanship, but I disagree. It's simply another skill, one that should be practiced and mastered. Some players have excellent strokes, some have great court speed and some make very effective line calls. It's just a matter of maximizing your talents.

Kibbitz Like the Pros
Kibbitz: To chat; to make small talk.

Unlike golf, tennis does not lend itself to creative kibbitzing. A round of golf can have numerous memorable shots, so after the round golfers will sit around and kid each other with good-natured comments such as, "Hey, Ben, remember that drive you hit on sixteen? That was the worst shot I've ever seen. It's like you never played the game before."

Then Ben says, "It's not as bad as the eighteen-inch putt you blew on eleven. A colony of mutant bacteria could've made that one." And so on.

However, a typical tennis match doesn't have many noteworthy shots, so the kibbitzing skills of tennis players tend to be rather weak. This is evidenced by the poor showing of tennis players in international kibbitzing tournaments. Quite often, tennis players finish dead last in this competition, which is (or should be) an embarrassment to us all. The reason is that most tennis players are not familiar with the proper techniques of effective kibbitzing. To help rectify this situation, I've included some basic tips below.

Be positive and assertive

Kibbitzing, like poaching, should be done with real conviction. After all, when you poach you don't just stick your racket out and hope the ball hits it, do you? (Well, you shouldn't.) You go after the ball, stepping forward as well as towards the middle. That's what you must do when kibbitzing.

For example, let's say your partner missed an easy putaway on an important point. In your post-match discussion you don't say, "Gosh, that was really bad luck you had on set point."

Instead you say, "Man, you choked on that overhead like a snake trying to swallow an alligator." (Which, by the way, happened in the Florida Everglades. A gigantic Burmese Python was discovered with a half-swallowed alligator in its mouth. The snake was dead, of course, but you have to admire that kind of ambition.)

Get technical

Quite often, tennis discussions focus on injuries, especially among veteran players. To kibbitz effectively in this area you should visit a few medical websites and pick up some technical terminology to toss into the conversation. Terms such as anterior cruciate ligament and lateral meniscus are good for starters.

A word of caution here, though. If there are doctors in your group they can make you look pretty foolish when you start throwing medical jargon around. It turns out that downloading a few tidbits of information off the Internet is not the same as graduating from medical school, going through residency, passing certification boards and practicing medicine.

Embellish your stories

When you kibbitz about your tennis stories, people aren't really interested in veracity so much as entertainment value. Don't be afraid to embellish heavily. For example, let's say you had a good win over a ranked player in a tournament. You can use a little dramatic license in describing the match, culminating in the leaping backhand overhead you hit for a winner on match point. Your tennis friends will know it's a crock, but they'll still be impressed just for the sake of a good kibbitz.

So there you have it, the basic techniques of effective kibbitzing. If you work on them faithfully and diligently, in no time at all you'll be kibbitzing like the pros.

The Unwritten Rules

There are a number of highly important, unwritten rules in tennis. They include the following:

Rule No. 1

Never ask people who are more than one-half level above you to play. Unfortunately, there are many individuals who do not abide by this rule and, on occasion, you will be asked to play by a lesser opponent. The reason they usually give is that, "You'd be really good for my game." Never mind that they are of no value to your game unless, of course, you're desperate for an ego boost. But really, how much satisfaction should a 4.5 player receive by trouncing a 3.5 player?

It's an awkward situation because, while you don't want to play with this person, you don't want to explicitly say so. There are ways to get out of it, although none are very gracious. Here are a few standard ones.

The "Can't you take a hint" series of excuses. It goes something like this. Let's say that a person you don't want to play with asks if you want to get together next Saturday.

> You say, "I can't, I already have a match."
>
> The person says, "How about Sunday?"
>
> You say, "Sorry, I have a match Sunday, too."
>
> The person says, "Well, what days are good for you next week?"
>
> You say, "I'm pretty booked for the next few weeks." Meanwhile you're thinking, *Geez, man, get a clue. Can't you see I don't want to play with you?*
>
> Finally the person says, "If you don't want to play with me just say so."
>
> You pretend to be offended and say, "Now what gave you that idea?" Then walk away in a huff.

Excuses so ridiculous that an idiot should be able to figure out they are totally bogus.

> "I can't play because I'm having my nipples pierced."
>
> "I can't play because I'm cleaning my computer chips."
>
> "I can't play because my wife gets out of prison that day and I have to pick her up."

The nuclear approach, i.e., brutal honesty.

This is where you respond to a request to play by saying,

"No thanks, I prefer to play with people at my own level." Many individuals will take this as a major put-down because they think their self-worth is measured by their tennis ability. This is nonsense. Tennis ability should not count for more than 60% of a person's self-worth. Attributes such as character, achievements and relationships are also important.

Regardless of what approach you take, you will get a reputation for being an arrogant schmuck who won't play with lower-level opponents. Other than not being the most popular person at your club, the only other significant effect will be that lesser players won't bother you anymore. Sometimes it pays to be a schmuck.

Rule No. 2

What happens on the tennis court doesn't stay on the tennis court. If you whiff an overhead, smash a racket or lose "love and love," be assured that your entire tennis world will know about it. Your only consolation is that you are free to relate all your opponents' embarrassing moments.

Rule No. 3

Grunting is prohibited unless a player hits the ball at least 30 mph. It's very deceiving, bordering on gamesmanship, when someone hits a dribbler that barely makes it over the net while bellowing like a rogue elephant.

Rule No. 4

Everyone's vision gets better when they are playing in a tournament. Not only do they see the ball better but, apparently, they also see the lines better because they make a lot closer "out" calls.

Rule No. 5

You should only take bathroom breaks when you're winning (unlike the pros).

Rule No. 6

If you bring the balls you can foot-fault. This actually is a semi-official rule at a club in central Florida, but it's kind of meaningless since many players foot-fault anyway.

Rule No. 7

If your opponent's first serve is well out, do not try and return the ball. Hit it into the bottom of the net or let it go behind you. Match play is not the time to practice your service return, and it's gamesmanship to intentionally disrupt a player's service rhythm.

If someone you play against does this regularly, you wouldn't be out of line mentioning it to them. If that doesn't work, then whenever they miss their first serve, hit a sky high lob and say, "Second serve." Yes, it's petty and juvenile and yes, you're lowering yourself to their level, but what the hell. It's for a good cause and it satisfies your inner jackass.

Rule No. 8

When you play with a new racket, your game improves because you are motivated to move better and watch the ball more closely. After a few weeks you return to your normal level as you lapse back into your old bad habits.

Rule No. 9

When you're playing well and winning, nothing bothers you. An alien spaceship could land on an adjacent court, drop off a pile of giant seedpods, then take off and, at most, you'd play a let.

Corollary to Rule No. 9

When you're playing badly and losing, everything bothers you. Somebody could open a can of balls three courts away, and you'd grit your teeth and silently scream, HOW CAN ANYONE PLAY WITH ALL THIS DAMN NOISE?

These differences are graphically displayed when a ball from your court rolls onto the court next to you during a point. The one who is winning just smiles as if to say, "No problem," and tosses the ball back. The one who is losing gives you a glare that says, "I'd like to rip out your liver and feed it to a pack of rabid wolves." (Tennis players can say a lot with just a look.)

Rule No. 10

When you go to the orthopedist for an injury, and the doctor asks if you want pain pills, always say yes and always get the maximum prescription. Sooner or later you're going to need it.

Rule No. 11

You always get hurt when you're playing really well.

Rule No. 12

Apparently, this a Hollywood rule. When you make a movie that includes tennis scenes, be sure to use actors that have absolutely no clue how to play the game. Also, have them take a lot of wild, uncoordinated swings, which look nothing like tennis strokes, so they look as ridiculous as possible.

Rule No. 13

Before stripping off your warm-up pants be sure you're wearing shorts underneath them. Hopefully, you haven't violated this rule but if you do (and you can take my word for this) people will never let you forget it.

A Non-Tennis Rule

Do not order grits in England.

Player Quotes

"It would have been better if I had won, but reaching the final was perfect."
Andy Murray

"I've been in the twilight of my career longer than most people have had careers."
Martina Navratilova

"I'd rather be No. 2 in Chile and No. 1 in the world."
Nicolas Massu

"This [defeat] has taught me a lesson, but I'm not sure what it is."
John McEnroe.

"As good as anybody not named Roger."
Andy Roddick, on his chances of winning the US Open

"Experience is a great advantage. The problem is that when you get the experience, you're too damned old to do anything about it."
Jimmy Connors

"There are hundreds of players just like her in America."
Tracy Austin, after beating 13-year-old Steffi Graf

"Sure, on a given day I could beat him [Ivan Lendl]. But it would have to be a day when he had food poisoning."
Former touring pro Mel Purcell

"Not yet. It's my first day on the job. Give me some time."
Marat Safin, on not breaking a racket during his first match of 2002

Chapter II

Take Two
(A pair of tennis tragedies)

Part 1
Tennis Interruptus
(Who needs weather anyway?)

10:00 PM, Tennis Eve

Here's the scenario. You injured your hamstring and haven't played tennis for over a month. It has been one of the bleakest periods of your life, but now, finally, you are able to play and you have a doubles match set up with your regular foursome at 5:00 PM tomorrow. You look forward to it with the same relish that a ravenous great white shark looks forward to a holiday weekend at a New England beach.

Only three things can prevent you from playing.

1) A meteor strike that wipes out all life on Earth

2) Someone in your group cancels

3) The weather

You've checked the science news and there is no imminent danger of a meteor collision. You've called everyone in the group multiple times, eventually eliciting responses such as, "Would you please stop calling me? My wife is starting to think I'm having an affair. For the tenth time, I *can* play tomorrow."

11:00 PM, Tennis Eve

That just leaves the weather, a fickle force of nature that can foil the firmest of tennis plans. So you go online, check four different weather sites and they all have the same forecast: Zero percent chance of precipitation and not a single rain blob on the local radar maps.

8:00 AM Tennis Day

You leap out of bed, look out the window and see nothing but clear blue sky and a warm, golden sun. Ecstatic, you climb into your car and drive to work.

9:00 AM Tennis Day

You roll into work and check your e-mail. You have 57 new ones and most are marked "urgent." You wade through your e-mail and do some paperwork, checking the weather every twenty minutes. Still looking great.

11:00 AM Tennis Day

You head for your weekly meeting, taking along your cell phone so you can keep tabs on the weather. At one point in the meeting the chairman asks you what you think of "the problem." What you think is, *I don't care if 'the problem' drives the company out of business, as long as I get to play tennis this afternoon.* Instead, you mumble something unintelligible and your co-workers give you looks that say, "What the hell are you on?"

12:00 PM Tennis Day

Since it's such a beautiful day, you decide to eat lunch outside. As you sit there munching away, you envision yourself playing exceptional tennis—scampering around the court, swatting groundstrokes, punching volleys and smashing overheads. You are quivering with anticipation.

1:00 PM Tennis Day

You head back to work, taking one last look at the beautiful blue sky. Then something disturbing catches your eye. Off to the west, just above the horizon line, is a thin, wispy cloud— make that two thin, wispy clouds. You rush inside to check the weather sites and the first two are still forecasting a zero percent chance of rain. However, the next two are now calling for a

10% chance at 5:00 PM. Plus, there are a couple of tiny green blobs on the radar maps. You start to hyperventilate, then you catch yourself and think, *Calm down, man. There is still a 90% chance it won't rain.*

2:00 PM Tennis Day

You know you have to stop thinking about the weather or you'll go nuts, so you sit down at your desk and try to do some actual work. Unfortunately, your mind is totally disengaged and you end up further behind than when you started.

3:00 PM Tennis Day

You go outside, look up and see that the thin wispy clouds have now become fluffy white ones, and there are quite few of them. You rush back in to check the weather sites and they are now calling for a 20 - 30% chance of rain. Also, the little green blobs have multiplied, grown larger and are heading straight for your area.

3:30 PM Tennis Day

You go outside again and see that the clouds are now a menacing gray. Plus, they are covering half the sky, just as a dark cloud is now covering half your brain. Then you hear it, the first distant rumble of thunder.

4:00 PM Tennis Day

With great trepidation, you recheck the weather sites and they are forecasting, WHAT? A 70% CHANCE OF RAIN! HOW CAN THIS HAPPEN? Also, the little green blobs have joined forces into one huge, ominous-looking blob that is about to engulf your area. You begin to panic and start making deals with God. "Lord," you say, "if you'll just hold off the rain until 6:30, I promise to go to church regularly, to tithe, to self-flagellate, anything you want."

"Hey guys, come back. I think it's letting up."

4:15 PM Tennis Day

The weather forecasts are now calling for a 90% chance of torrential rain.

4:30 PM Tennis Day

You go outside one last time and watch as lightning tears across the sky, followed by a tremendous clap of thunder, as if God is saying, "I've heard this before and I don't believe it. Fool me once, shame on you. Fool me twice, you're toast."

5:00 PM Tennis Day

The lightning and thunder are now putting on a dazzling, non-stop show. The sky is as black as midnight, and the towering storm clouds are saturated with an ocean of water. Suddenly the heavens open up and a torrent gushes forth, inundating the earth like a Biblical plague. One of your co-workers makes a brilliant observation. "Boy, it's really coming down out there," he says. Somehow, you resist the urge to strangle him.

5:30 PM Tennis Day

As you sit at your desk, disconsolately, your wife calls, and the conversation goes like this:

"Hello," you say.

"Hi, hon," she says sympathetically. "The weather's pretty bad. I guess you're kind of bummed that you can't play."

More like suicidal, you think, but instead you say, "Yeah, a little."

"Well, don't get too down," she says. "Tomorrow is supposed to be nice."

"Is it really?" you ask, wondering if your wife is in on this monstrous conspiracy.

"That's what I heard," she says. "Anyhow, since

you can't play tonight why don't we go out to eat? You pick the restaurant."

"How about one in the Sahara Desert or Death Valley," you respond. "Any place where it never rains."

She laughs and says, "I'm glad to see you're taking this so well."

Part 2

The Tournament Player
(A tennis melodrama in one act)

Characters in order of appearance:
1) THE PLAYER
2) REALITY
3) THE INTERNET
4) THE SPOUSE
5) THE OPPONENT

(THE PLAYER enters and addresses the audience.)

THE PLAYER

Well, I did it. I signed up for my first tournament. As of now I am a battle-hardened soldier of the tennis wars. At least I will be after I play an actual match. Y'know, I really need to look into buying a trophy display case. Maybe two.

(REALITY enters.)

REALITY

What you really need to do is dial it back a little.

THE PLAYER

How so?

REALITY

You haven't even played the first round of your first tournament and already you're shopping for trophy cases. Shouldn't you be getting prepared for your match tomorrow?

THE PLAYER

You're right, I should. Let's see now. First, I'll put all my rackets into plastic wrappers and label the tensions with sticky notes.

REALITY

You have two rackets and you don't know the tension of either one. Why don't you concentrate on your evening meal.

THE PLAYER

Right again. Isn't carbo-loading the accepted regimen? But I heard that carbs are bad and protein is good. Or is it the other way around? I kind of lost track. What do you think?

REALITY

I'm not sure either. Go ask THE INTERNET.

(THE PLAYER walks into the computer room.)

THE PLAYER
INTERNET!

THE INTERNET
Yo!

THE PLAYER

INTERNET, please tell me. Is it carbs bad and protein good or the other way around?

THE INTERNET
Yes and no.

THE PLAYER
What do you mean?

THE INTERNET

I mean I have sites that say both, so tell me what answer you're looking for. Just make it quick; I was chatting with a hot Asian teen who has low mortgage rates.

THE PLAYER
I don't know the answer. That's why I'm asking you.

THE INTERNET
Look, I tell people what they want to hear. If you don't know what you want, it's your problem.

THE PLAYER
That isn't very helpful.

THE INTERNET
Hey, you came to me. If you don't like my answer go do your research in a book store, if you can still find one.

THE PLAYER
Do you have any suggestions for an evening meal?

THE INTERNET
I'm getting a lot of positive input on dark chocolate and red wine.

THE PLAYER
That sounds good. Okay, what's next?

REALITY
I should think a good night's sleep is important.

THE PLAYER
Definitely. A good night's sleep is an absolute imperative. INTERNET, do you have anything on that?

THE INTERNET
About thirty million sites. Here's a good one.

(THE PLAYER sits down at the computer and begins to read.)

THE PLAYER (Reading)

Tips for getting restful sleep. Step one: Do not put pressure on yourself by saying things like, "A good night's sleep is an absolute imperative." Well, that's not a good start. I'll skip to the next step. Actually, I should be lying in bed while reading this so I'll print it out.

(THE PLAYER prints out a few pages, walks into the bedroom, gets into his PJs and hops into bed. Then he continues reading.)

THE PLAYER

Step 2: Do not read or watch television in bed. Okay, we'll skip step two.

Step 3: Turn off all lights and block windows with blackout shades to get your room as dark as possible. That's zero for three. I'll just have to get to sleep on my own.

(THE PLAYER puts the pages on the dresser and turns out the light. For the next two hours he sleeps only a few minutes because something is nagging at him. Eventually, he sits up.)

THE PLAYER

There's something important I've forgotten.

REALITY

You should look at the draw to see what time you play.

THE PLAYER

Right. Y'know, you could have told me this earlier.

REALITY

I wanted to teach you a lesson.

THE PLAYER
Must you always do that?

REALITY
Yes.

(THE PLAYER gets out of bed and pads to the computer room.)

THE PLAYER
INTERNET!

THE INTERNET
What now?

THE PLAYER
Go to the tournament website and tell me what time I'm playing. Do NOT tell me *who* I'm playing.

THE INTERNET
Shouldn't that be *whom* you're playing?

THE PLAYER
Whatever. Just do it.

THE INTERNET
Okay. Looks like you're playing at 9:00 AM. Uh oh.

THE PLAYER
Uh oh, what?

THE INTERNET
You don't want to know. It will make you even more nervous, and you certainly don't need that.

THE PLAYER

I'm already nervous about the "uh oh" so go ahead and tell me.

INTERNET

You're playing the number two seed. Want me to look up his record?

THE PLAYER

I guess.

THE INTERNET

Whoa!

THE PLAYER

What?

THE INTERNET

Are you sure you want to know?

THE PLAYER

No, but tell me anyway.

THE INTERNET

He's the number four ranked player in the state and he has won some pretty big tournaments.

THE PLAYER

Thanks for the info.

THE INTERNET

Look on the bright side. At least you'll have the rest of the weekend free.

THE PLAYER
Go stuff it, you chip-for-brains.

(THE PLAYER returns to bed and for the next four hours cannot get to sleep. Finally, at around 4:00 AM, he falls asleep. The alarm rings at 7:00 AM. THE SPOUSE prods him awake.)

THE SPOUSE
Time to get up, hon. You have a big match this morning.

(THE PLAYER slowly gets up.)

THE SPOUSE
You don't look so good. How do you feel?

THE PLAYER
Like a zombie on Valium.

(THE PLAYER drags himself out of bed, takes a quick shower, gets dressed and gulps down a cup of coffee. Then he drives to the tennis courts, parks and walks over to the registration desk where THE OPPONENT is waiting. He introduces himself.)

THE PLAYER
Hi, I'm THE PLAYER.

THE OPPONENT
Nice to meet you, I'm THE OPPONENT. We're on court three. I have the balls.

(They walk to the court and THE PLAYER notices the singles sticks, which make the net look about a foot higher. They begin the warm-up.)

THE PLAYER

This guy doesn't seem that good. He doesn't hit very hard or with a lot of spin. On the other hand, he hasn't missed a shot and hits every ball within three feet of the baseline.

(The match begins. One hour later the match ends.)

THE PLAYER

It's amazing how quickly you can go from a conquering hero in your mind to cannon fodder on the court. I lost 6-2, 6-1 and didn't play all that badly. THE OPPONENT had an answer for everything I did, but I learned a few things:

1) Tournament competition is serious and intense.

2) My second serve is a sitting duck for an accomplished player.

3) I can hold off on those trophy cases.

REALITY

Welcome to my world.

Commentator Quotes

"If this match were being played on water, Roddick would be drowning while Federer would be walking on it."
Chris Bailey, BBC

"Winners win."
Justin Gimelstob (a.k.a., Captain Obvious)

"Michael Chang is now playing his own game… and he does that better than anyone."
Christine Janes

"That shot knocked the stuffing out of his sails!"
Frew McMillan

"Half come to see him win. Half come to see him lose. Half come to see what happens."
Ion Tiriac, talking about John McEnroe

"Laura Robson… solid between the ears."
Virginia Wade

"He [Andy Roddick] doesn't make mistakes, except when he has to."
Andrew Castle

"It's quite clear that Virginia Wade is thriving on the pressure now that the pressure on her to do well is off."
Harry Carpenter

"His two greatest strengths are his legs, his speed, his agility and his competitiveness."
Pat Cash on Lleyton Hewitt

**Taking practice swings in your
home is fraught with danger.**

Chapter III

Musings from No-Man's Land
(The sordid and the assorted)

Tennis Addiction Syndrome (TADS)
The Warning Signs

At the present time, TADS is not considered by the American Psychiatric Association to be a treatable disorder (although it should be because damn near every other aspect of human behavior is). Nevertheless, avid tennis players know this is a very real condition. To help people determine if they have this syndrome, the warning signs of TADS are listed below.

- You have more tennis partners than family members on speed dial and group texting.

- When you can't play for over a week, you have to be put on suicide watch.

- When you plan a vacation, the first thing you check on is the location of area tennis courts.

- You've named a pet after a racket company.

- You have more tennis fantasies than erotic ones.

- You have enough tennis balls in your car (which looks and smells like a locker room) to start your own academy.

- You've injured one family member and broken at least three objects while taking practice swings in your home.

- You have two categories of Facebook™ friends: "Tennis" and "Others."

- You've slept with a new racket.

- You hang out at tennis shops on rainy days.

- You intentionally hold your toothbrush with a semi-Western grip.

- Most of the greeting cards you receive are tennis related.

- You use the Tennis Channel as background sound for romantic encounters.

- You wake up at 3:00 AM in a cold sweat, wondering if you should increase your string tension by two pounds.

- You can trace your life history by the rackets you've used.

- You get off on the sound and the smell of opening a can of balls.

- Your significant other says, "You love tennis more than me," and you have to think about it before responding.

If you exhibit fewer than eight of these warning signs, you are spending way too much time *not* playing tennis. Clearly, your priorities are out of whack.

The Brain of a Tennis Player
Just as we suspected

Recent advances in neuroscience have confirmed that the brain of a tennis player, unlike the brain of a normal person, is divided into only two lobes:

- A large, primary lobe that is dedicated solely to tennis

- A much smaller, secondary lobe that handles all other aspects of life

The secondary lobe functions remarkably well, considering the relatively small amount of brainpower it is allotted. However, it must shut down completely when the primary lobe, which always gets top priority, starts commandeering brain cells to deal with a tennis crisis.

The following is an example of this situation.

Let's say you just finished a match and you're on your way to the grocery store. Overall, you played pretty well but you really struggled with your backhand. You weren't hitting it with your usual authority and many of your shots were landing way too short.

When you get to the grocery you park your car, grab a cart and head into the store. However, your mind is totally engrossed with your backhand problems. You wander aimlessly through the aisles while trying out various practice strokes, oblivious to the fact that you've toppled over several floor displays and bruised a lot of fruit.

In addition, you pay no attention to your shopping list and simply toss random items into the cart. You eventually reach the checkout line and, as you do, it suddenly dawns on you what you were doing wrong. You were using a shortened backswing, which meant you couldn't generate enough racket head speed for an effective shot. You take a few strokes with a longer backswing and notice that they feel really good, especially when you knock one of the bagboys into an adjacent checkout aisle.

Elated, you pay for your groceries, load them into your car and drive home. When you arrive, you pile the bags on the counter and your wife (or husband/mom/roommate) starts pulling out items, horrified at what they find. "WHAT THE HELL IS ALL THIS CRAP?" they scream. "You didn't get anything that was on the list! Where was your head? Still on the tennis court, I'll bet."

However, all that sound and fury doesn't bother you in the slightest because you're pretty sure you've solved your backhand problem. So it's all good, even if you do have to eat pickled pig's brains for the next few weeks.

Lefties and Normies

(Note to the lefties: The following might come off as a negative depiction of left-handed tennis players. If that's what you conclude, you're not being paranoid.)

I'm not suggesting that being a left-handed tennis player is inherently wrong, nor do I condone the idea that lefties should be rounded up, put into tennis re-education camps and taught to play like normal, right-handed people (a.k.a., normies.)

But if you do some research on the subject, you will find that historically left-handedness was considered to be an extremely negative trait in many cultures. The Latin word "sinistra" originally meant "left" but took on meanings of "evil" or "unlucky." This double meaning survives in the English word "sinister." That's not me talking, that's etymology.

And what is it about playing lefties that we normies do not like? Two things primarily…

1) The slice serve in the ad court that takes a normie way out of position.

2) The high-kicking, topspin forehand to a normie's backhand.

The question is, how do we righties overcome these natural, yet sinister lefty advantages?

(Note: If you are a lefty please stop reading here.)

1) To counteract the wide-swinging serve, step in and rip a flat, down-the-line backhand that lands just inside both the sideline and baseline.

2) For the topspin lefty forehand, take the ball on the rise, and hit a wicked crosscourt slice that lands at about the service line and carries well off the court.

Of course, if you could actually execute such shots consistently you'd be on the pro tour or playing top-level age group tournaments instead of reading a silly tennis book. For the rest of us, I suggest a lot of moon balls, drop shots and sky-high lobs. You might not win but at the very least, lefties will never play with you again.

Net Cord vs. Let Cord

There are two kinds of people in the tennis world. Those who use the term "net-cord" to describe a ball that hits the top of the net, and those who use the term "let-cord." Like dog people and cat people, net-cord people and let-cord people will never come to an agreement, yet they can still co-exist as long as they abide by the golden rule of tennis: Do unto others, even if you think they're idiots for using incorrect tennis terminology, as you would have them do unto you.

As for the net-cord/let-cord debate, neither one is really right. "Net-cord" is a misnomer because the term is already used as the name of the wire that holds up the net. Neither is "let-cord" appropriate because a ball that hits the top of the net is not a let unless it's a serve.

Of the two, net-cord is a better choice but there is one caveat. "Let" is derived from a shortening of the word "filet," the French expression for "net." So technically, when we say let-cord we really mean net-cord.

There are two conclusions that can be drawn...
   1)   Either net-cord or let-cord is acceptable
   2)   This was a pretty useless discussion.

The Mixed Tennis Marriage

A mixed tennis marriage is defined as a union wherein partner *A* is an avid tennis player (We'll assume *A* is a male) and partner *B* is an avid non-tennis player. (Obviously, *B* is a female, although it could be another male; we're not judging here. And yes, partner

A could have been female and *B* male, or *B* another female. But that's not the point! Sheesh!) Anyhow, partners *A* and *B*, whatever they are, have diametrically opposite objectives in life.

A's primary objective is to play as much tennis as possible, and *B's* primary objective is to make his life a living hell for doing so. One might ask how people with such contradictory purposes can sustain a harmonious union. The answer is that the relationship works because it rests on one of the three pillars necessary for a long and healthy marriage—mutual pretense. This can be seen in a typical Saturday morning conversation between *A* and *B* as shown below. (Note: Beneath the spoken words is the actual meaning of the conversation.)

A: It's supposed to be a beautiful today.
(I have a 9:00 AM tennis match.)

B: Good, then you can help me pull weeds.
(Let's start the guilt trip.)

A: That's not exactly what I had in mind.
(You know I'm playing tennis.)

B: And just what did you have in mind?
(As if I didn't know.)

A: I was thinking of playing a little tennis.
(I was thinking of playing a LOT of tennis.)

B: So I get to work while you have fun?
(Typical.)

A: Fun? You think chasing a ball around in this heat is fun?
(Actually, it is.)

B: So why do you do it?
(Why DO you do it?)

A: (heading out the door) Someone has to.

(Side note: In case you're wondering about the other two pillars of a long and happy marriage, and I speak from many years of experience, they are communication and togetherness. You must avoid these at all costs. If husbands and wives start hanging out and talking more than is absolutely necessary, pretty soon one or both will be thinking, *Why the hell did I marry this yahoo?* Next thing you know, someone turns up missing and the spouse is on *Dateline* or *48 Hours.* Happens all the time.)

But back to the mixed tennis marriage. It is obvious that *A* and *B* have to work out an arrangement whereby both their needs are satisfied. One idea that has worked for numerous couples is known as the Credit System. In this scheme, *A* performs a variety of tasks specified by *B*, and earns "tennis credits" in the process. The credits are cashed in at a standard value of ten credits per set.

Here are some examples:

1) Doing the laundry: 5 credits, with a 3-credit bonus for separating whites and coloreds.
(Caution: Bras do not go in the dryer.)

2) Taking the kids for the day: 10 credits
(If you have kids.)

3) Bringing them home safely: 20 credits
(Unless you don't have kids.)

4) Executing a particularly erotic maneuver while wearing a Zorro costume: 25 credits

Of course, there is a negative side to this system, such as:

1) Forgetting a birthday or anniversary: 10-credit deduction

2) Remembering a birthday or anniversary but getting vacuum cleaner bags as a present: 20-credit deduction

3) Using "Pudge-muffin" as a pet name: 50-credit
deduction plus loss of marital privileges

In conclusion, a mixed tennis marriage can work, it just takes a lot of pretense, deception and deal-making, as do all successful marriages.

From the Glitter to the Gutter
The tragic lives of tennis balls

Like triplets bursting from their pressurized cocoon, tennis balls come into the world full of hope and promise. Glittering with an aura of iridescent yellow and gushing with youthful exuberance, they fairly leap into your hands eager to be put in play.

When the match commences they soar gleefully about the court, fulfilling at last their manifest destiny. They bounce and skip and spin, as joyful as toddlers frolicking on a sun-drenched playground.

Then, as abruptly as it began, the match is over. You gather up the balls but it's obvious their youthful glow is gone. Although battered and worn they still retain a shred of vitality, and even seem to be pleading with you, "Please don't toss us into the bag with the old balls. Put us back in the can. We still have enough life for another match, or at least a practice session."

So you put them back in the can and use them a time or two for hitting practice, but soon they must go into the bag where they are demoted to the next level—wall balls. While the monotonous back and forth on the wall doesn't have the brio of match play, the aging balls are still giving all they have, and still giving you exercise and stroke practice.

Soon, however, they are too flat even for wall balls and are demoted again, this time to the hopper for serving practice. All they can look forward to now is the occasional smack of a serve, a one-time event with no competitive aspect. After a short time at this level they become so dingy and flat that they have no tennis value at all, so they are passed down to small children, sometimes even to dogs. These once-proud artifacts of a grand athletic contest have been reduced to mere playthings for tykes and animals.

Eventually, they are too worn and tattered even for that purpose, so they are ingloriously tossed in the garbage. Then the garbage is taken to the gutter and the old, dead balls are hauled off with the rest of the trash. There is no one to shed a tear nor to mourn their passing, no one to say a few parting words, such as, "Goodbye, little round ones and thanks for a job well done. You have served us admirably."

So the next time you finish a match, won't you take a moment to express your gratitude to our fuzzy friends who ask so little yet give so much? Just do it quietly or people will think you're freakin' nuts.

Wall Versed

When you hit against the wall, your mind tends to wander into various topics. Some people use this time to work out major problems in their lives, while others are inspired to create poetry that is:

Cheesy
I hit a ball
Against a wall
It came right back
This wall's no hack

Cheesier
Forehand, backhand
It matters not
The wall returns
My every shot

Cheesiest
The wall is stern
The wall is strong
It's there whene'er
My strokes go wrong

It's not the Racket, Stupid
Maybe it is

Today's tennis rackets are marvels of engineering design
and materials technology. They are light and maneuverable and
can generate considerable power and spin with very little effort.
Unfortunately, they have one major flaw: They are all highly
inconsistent. At least all the rackets that I've ever used are.

For example, I'll be out playing one day and my racket will
be extremely sharp, hitting the corners with good pace and laser-
like precision. The next day it can barely keep the ball in the
court. There's only one way to explain these extreme variations
in racket performance—inadequate quality control procedures
at the fabricating plants.

I don't understand why this should be the case because
with the advent of computer-aided manufacturing, these plants
should be able to crank out much more reliable products.
Furthermore, they undoubtedly have expert racket testers
evaluate their products for consistency and playability. Therein,
I believe, lies the problem. The testers are probably pros, former
pros and instructors who could play pretty good tennis with
a soup ladle. What they really need are people like me to test
their rackets.

However, since I haven't been asked to do so, I am planning
to conduct my own racket-testing program. If I have to play
every day for the rest of my life, if I have to spend every cent I
have in the world, I will continue my quest to find the perfect

stick. Call me a dreamer, call me a fool, better yet, call me if you have a racket to recommend.

Friends vs. Tennis Friends
There's a difference

- If you get sent to prison your friends will visit you. Your tennis friends will visit you and ask if you want to sell your rackets for half price.

- When you pass away your friends will come to your funeral and mourn for you. Your tennis friends will come to your funeral as long as it doesn't interfere with their match schedule.

- If you fall your friends will help you up. Your tennis friends will demand to play a let if they missed a shot while you were falling.

- If you lose your job your friends will offer assistance. Your tennis friends will let you slide on bringing the balls… for one match.

- If you get elected president of the US your friends will congratulate you. Your tennis friends will want to know how it affects your availability for league play.

- If you get impeached your friends will commiserate with you. Your tennis friends will want to know how it affects your availability for league play.

- If you get lost in the woods and call your friends on your cell phone, they will organize a search party. Your tennis friends will tell you to find a sub.

- If you get divorced your friends will ask how you are doing. Your tennis friends will ask if they can partner with your ex-husband or ex-wife if they play well.

- If you develop a drinking problem your friends will help you through it. Your tennis friends will buy you a few rounds.

- If you change careers and become a mob hitman, your friends will avoid you. Your tennis friends will also avoid you… after getting an estimate for knocking off their chief rivals.

Moments of Madness
Of angels and demons

I was in Atlanta (which, BTW, is a *great* tennis town) visiting friends who lived on the top floor of a high-rise. They had an open-air balcony that afforded a beautiful view of the city, and when everyone went out on the balcony to enjoy the view, I stayed inside. When asked why, I explained that I have vertigo and tend to get very dizzy in high, open places.

However, the real reason I wouldn't join the party was out of fear that I would have a moment of madness and take a flying leap off the balcony. I say this because I've had just such moments on a tennis court and, based on my experience, so have a lot of people. These moments are when we decide to hit a full-blown smash off a ball that bounces near the back fence, or hit a drop volley off a heavy topspin ball at our shoe-tops.

Why we try these ridiculous shots is a mystery, but here's one theory. We all have these opposing forces in our brains— the proverbial angels and demons. The angels tell us to hit shots within our capability and the demons tell us to go for the most difficult shots possible. Fortunately, we listen to the angels most of the time, but every once in awhile, we take the demonic path and have our moments of madness.

Now imagine you're on a balcony and you hear a voice that says, "Go ahead and jump; you can fly." It's the same voice you hear and occasionally obey when it tells you, "Go ahead and hit that backhand topspin lob; you can make it." Do you really want to take that chance?

The Camera Lies

If you ever decide it's a good idea for someone to shoot a video of you while you're playing a match, trust me, it's not. I speak from bitter experience on this topic because I did just that at a tennis camp. When I first saw myself on video, I thought, "Who is *that* bumbling doofus? It sure as hell can't be me." Yet he looked an awful lot like me—the same build, the same facial features, the same racket, even the same backwards cap. (It was at this moment when I realized that anyone over the age of nineteen who wears a cap that way looks a little silly, pros included.)

While the guy in the video may have *appeared* to be me, he certainly didn't *play* like me. He was late getting his racket back, he was hitting off his back foot and he was lumbering around like a pregnant hippo. I, on the other hand, am quite sure I look like that Swiss guy who moves around the court effortlessly and is in position for virtually every shot.

That evening, as I was trying to reconcile the cognitive dissonance between my mind's eye and the video camera, I happened upon the Science Channel, which was airing a show about parallel universes. One idea that caught my interest was that while our universe is dominated by particles, a parallel universe might be dominated by anti-particles. "Aha!" I thought. "That's the answer!" At the precise time when the video was shot, there was a tear in the space-time continuum that allowed the anti-me from a parallel universe to insinuate himself into the video. And since I do everything right, the anti-me does everything wrong.

To conclude, I learned two things from this experience:
1) Never underestimate the power of self-delusion.
2) Never be in a tennis video.

Devil Bugs

In various locations throughout North America, particularly near aquatic areas, there exists a species of insects specifically adapted to feed on tennis players. With the scientific name of *Ceratopogonidae Culicoides,* they are tiny little buggers you can barely see, hence the nickname, no-see-ums. Despite their diminutive size, *Culicoides* can bite the living hell out of you, hence the other nickname, flying teeth. (Actually, it's the blood-sucking females that do all the biting. Sexist jokes aside, they are attracted to the exhaled carbon dioxide.)

There are a number of effective repellants for this insect, one of them being, oddly enough, Avon Skin-So-Soft. However, this product has a perfume scent which can create a problem if your significant other is a not a tennis player. The problem is that you'll come home from your match smelling better than when you left. So you should probably apprise your SO of this situation before you leave the house. Otherwise, you could have a lot of explaining to do, especially if you play really well and come home a little too happy.

High on Tennis
Altitude-wise, that is

Playing at altitude (at least one mile in elevation) is the same as playing at lower levels except for two small differences:
1) You can't keep the ball in the court.
2) You can't breathe because the air is so thin. ("How thin is it?" you ask. It's so thin you can count the oxygen molecules in one breath... on one hand.)

Depending on how high you are (again, altitude-wise) it takes a few days to a week in order to get fully acclimated. When you return to near sea-level, you also have two problems:

1) You can't hit the ball past the service line.

2) You still can't breathe because the air is so thick it feels like you're sucking down Jell-O™ shots.

Speaking of which, there are numerous recipes for Jell-O shots but they are all variations of the basic one below. (Caution: Do not read the following if you are under 21 years of age. That works, right?)

Jell-O shot recipe…

Jell-O powder
(Any flavor. They all have the same effect.)

Water (In moderation)

Vodka (In immoderation)

Mix, chill, slurp. Repeat as required.

(Note: Recipe is suitable for any elevation.)

Tennis Hell

We'd all like to believe in the idea of ultimate justice, wherein the good will be rewarded and the wicked punished. (Which is understandable since most of us put ourselves in the "good" category.) The tennis world is no different, so for those people who deserve it and, in my experience it's a very small number, here are your opponents for all eternity:

Level 1: Grinders who never miss on slow, slippery clay courts.

Level 2: Monster servers who can't hit two shots in a row on lightning fast courts.

Level 3: Beginners who don't even know the rules on cracked cement courts.

Level 4: Satan himself on flaming brimstone courts. (It turns out that Satan plays exactly like Fabrice Santoro, who was Marat Safin's idea of a tennis hell opponent.)

In addition, there's always a 40 mph wind blowing, the only thing to drink is warm Gatorade and the guy with the leaf-blower is right next to your court.

Tennis Heaven

Many people picture tennis heaven as a place where you always play your best, you always win and the conditions are always perfect. But I question that concept. For one thing, only half the people in tennis heaven can win, so where do the losers come from? Do they bus them in from tennis hell, or is there a tennis limbo from which the cannon fodder is drawn? Tennis theology can be a very complex matter.

Personally, I can't imagine a better place to play for all eternity than right here. If you're playing with your friends, having competitive but amiable matches, isn't that as good as it gets? Besides, people who have near-death experiences all talk about seeing bright lights, and I hate playing at night.

The Psycho Game
Someone is not with the program

Originally, this segment was going to be named "The Psychological Game," but since tennis can make you a little crazy, the above title seemed more appropriate. After all, in what other area of your life do you berate yourself so harshly? Maybe it happens when you smash your toe on the leg of the coffee table, even though you've walked past it ten thousand times. But really, you deserve to be chastised for that. It's not like the damn thing moves. But I digress.

Whenever I scream at myself on a tennis court for some bonehead shot or see others do so, I wonder what part of the brain is in control at that point. It can't be a part that is engaged in executing tennis commands because if that were the case it would be screaming at itself. No, it must be a rogue band of neurons that has separated itself from the rest of our brains and is telling us what we are doing wrong. We'll call them Supervisory Neurons.

If this hypothesis holds water, the Supervisory Neurons must confer on us a significant survival benefit. So let us return to the dawn of our species approximately 200,000 years ago. The males of that period, just as is true of males today, were primarily involved with impressing females. However, instead of driving too fast or drinking too much beer, they had to use their available opportunities, such as wrestling saber-toothed tigers.

In a fight between a 700-pound apex predator with 18-inch fangs, and a two-legged Happy Meal™, you'd have to bet on the tiger. However, there must have been a few males around who had the beneficial mutation of Supervisory Neurons and, when they thought about taking on a saber-tooth, the neurons said, "That's a really bad idea, dude." So they refrained from doing so and not only survived but usually got the girl because the tiger-wrestling males didn't live very long.

Sounds pretty far-fetched, I know, but consider this. There are those few golden times in our lives when we play our absolute best tennis. We are locked in and totally focused. We feel as if we can get to every ball and hit it exactly where we want it to go. We move effortlessly and watch the ball intently, and when we do make an error we never criticize ourselves. Now what do you suppose is happening? I submit to you that our Supervisory

Neurons have decided to join the rest of the neurons in the task at hand. Our entire brains are concentrated on playing tennis, so naturally we play our best.

As for why this happens only on rare occasions, no one can say. Perhaps the Supervisory Neurons are messing with our heads, which wouldn't be difficult since they're already in there. It does lead to an intriguing possibility. Suppose we could harness and control the Supervisory Neurons such that they are always in sync with the rest of our brains, meaning that we would always play our best tennis. Would that not be a tantalizing scenario?

However, there is a downside. Our Supervisory Neurons would no longer be warning us when we are about to do something self-destructive. Instead of wrestling with vicious animals that are no longer around, we might start picking fights with 300-pound bikers, or we might be inclined to call a foot-fault on Serena Williams during a Grand Slam match.

Nevertheless, if neurological advances can accomplish the feat of uniting our brains, then one day, as a male tennis player, you could be faced with the ultimate existential question: How many years of your life would you sacrifice to play your best tennis all the time?

As for female tennis players, if they decided to use male tennis players as their pool of potential mates, they would have two choices:

1) Males who play consistently well but have very little chance of long-term survival

2) Males who play erratically but will likely live a long time.

My guess is that most females will go with the first option, and purchase life insurance policies that pay triple for death by monumental stupidity.

Bloodsport
Husband and Wife Mixed Doubles

When we walk onto a tennis court our primary objective is to win the match. We all know it's not supposed to be a matter of life and death, and we all know we're supposed to play for the love of the sport. But let's face it, our main goal is to win. The exception is when we're playing a husband and wife doubles team. In that case our main goal is to seriously damage, if not destroy, the marriage of the opposing couple.

If we can get them saying words such as child custody, division of property and restraining order we will have accomplished our objective. In the process we will almost assuredly win the match, but that's just gravy. The meat, potatoes and two sides of the effort are undermining the relationship.

So how do we go about doing this? We follow two simple rules.

1) We don't play with our spouses. This is not an absolute rule because you may be one of those extremely rare couples who can not only play well together but can also keep your emotions off the court. Good luck with that.

2) We let the woman hit all the putaways and sitters she can, making sure she tries to nail the opposing man, preferably in a vital area. If he's a decent player he'll reflex a few winners, but eventually she's going to stick him good. This will enrage him, at least momentarily, because no man, no matter how liberated, can handle getting nailed by a woman. Naturally, he will blame it on his wife and give her either a dirty look or a verbal reprimand. This will enrage her, and before you can say, "I'm calling my lawyer!" both their tennis games and their marriage will begin to disintegrate.

Husband and wife doubles can create tension in a marriage.

At this point some readers must be thinking, *How can anyone possibly take pleasure in breaking up a marriage? That's just awful.* On the surface it would seem so, but think about it this way. If their relationship cannot stand up to the pressures of mixed doubles, how is it going to stand up to the pressures of life? The answer is, it won't, and by breaking up the marriage now we are saving them from years of bitterness and recrimination. In reality, we're performing a valuable service. Plus, it's so much fun.

Giggle Tennis
Definition: Playing with beginners
while pretending to enjoy it.

There are two situations in which you could get trapped into playing Giggle Tennis.

1) Family gatherings. You can usually get out of this one with a flimsy excuse or by being so obnoxious when you do play, they never ask you again.

2) The workplace. This one is tougher because some tool in HR has convinced upper management that it would be a great team-building experience for the whole workforce to go out and play tennis together. Naturally, they want the serious players to team up with the novices so they can bring the overall level up. But that's not what happens. The beginners bring the level down, such that the tennis, if you can even call it that, is abysmal.

If you're one of the better players, which, in this case, means you know how to keep score, you not only have to play but you have to make it look as though you're enjoying yourself. If you beg off or cop an attitude on the court you will get a reputation for not being a "team player" (a.k.a., political suck-up), and not being a team player is about the worst rep you can have.

The only way to survive "giggle tennis."

You could be the most creative, productive employee in the place, as individualists often are, but if you're not considered a team player you'll go nowhere. In fact, being competent at your job is an almost sure way of not getting promoted. All those team players in management certainly don't want to compete with someone who has actual talent.

So how do you get through the ordeal of Giggle Tennis without becoming suicidal? One word—alcohol. Normally, it is not a good idea to imbibe before going out to play, but in Giggle Tennis it's a necessity. If you don't or can't drink, then you have to find a substitute—herbal or prescription, legal or illicit—it doesn't matter as long as you get your head right and into your happy place.

The tennis will still be horrible but if you're properly medicated you won't give a damn. Furthermore, you'll look like you're having such a good time people will point to you and say, "Now *that* is a team player!"

Brain-Dead at Forty-Love

When you're playing a sport in which the game score can get into the forties (football and basketball come to mind), a 40-point lead is considered to be insurmountable. However, in tennis, when the game reaches forty-love, although it's really just 3-0, the Byzantine nature of the scoring system transports the server into a state of delusional euphoria.

If you're the server you feel as if you're so far ahead that you have an uncontrollable urge to go for some classic brain-dead shots. To wit…

How about sneaking into the net behind a short floater to your opponent's rocket-like forehand? Yeah, man!

Or trying a drop-shot from ten feet behind the baseline? Capital idea!

Wait a minute, I know! What about a behind-the-back volley? Definitely!

And so it goes. Someday, when the nations of the world come together in peace and harmony, and the tennis powers come together and abandon this absurd scoring system for a rational one, all such madness will cease.

Until then, keep trying that swinging backhand volley at forty-love. After all, you're up by forty points, how can you lose?

Stats for the Rest of Us

The statistics for a professional match include such categories as winners, unforced errors, percentage of serves won, and so forth. For average players these stats aren't really appropriate, not to mention the fact that they'd be pretty ugly. So here are a few that might be more fitting. The groupings are winners and mistakes. (Note: Mistakes are not necessarily outright errors, just really bad shots that will almost certainly lose the point.) Let's start with winners, of which there are six subgroups…

I meant to do that winners

This category is for really great shots that you actually tried to hit. It's not for an easy putaway, it's for shots like a low volley that you angle out of your opponent's reach, or a ripped groundstroke you hit from way behind the baseline. These are the shots you savor for a few moments, then store in your non-volatile memory to be played back at times when life gets you down, such as when you get a letter from the IRS saying they want to talk to you ASAP. You envision the shot and think, *Yes, I might get indicted for income tax evasion, but damn that was a great volley.*

Another good time to recall your best shots is when you're on a airplane that is about to leave the terminal. Like all the other passengers, you're trying very hard *not* to think about all the things that can go wrong with the plane. So what happens? The flight attendant gets on the speaker and *tells* you, in lurid detail, all the things that can go wrong.

I especially enjoy the part where they say, "In the event of a decompression, an oxygen mask will automatically appear in front of you. To start the flow of oxygen, pull the mask towards you. Place it firmly over your nose and mouth, secure the elastic band behind your head, and breathe normally." Right. With people screaming and oxygen masks flying around, I'm guessing there will be a lot of abnormal breathing.

I did not mean to do that winners
A typical scenario for this category is when your opponent hits a deep approach shot to your backhand. On the dead run, you decide, for some unfathomable reason, to try the most difficult shot possible—a cross court passing shot with heavy topspin. You catch it late and, instead of going crosscourt, the ball goes straight down the line for a winner. If no one is around, you hold your hand up because your opponent knows you didn't intend that shot. However, if anyone is watching, you nonchalantly stroll back into position for the next point as if to say, "Yep, I meant to do that." It's always acceptable to take credit for winners when people are watching.

So bad they're good winners
These are shots you play about as badly as possible. You don't move your feet, you don't get your racket back and you don't watch the ball. You just take a half-hearted slap at it, whereupon the ball dribbles off your racket frame then splats on the opponent's side like a bug on a windshield, usually for a winner. These shots are so bad that when you raise your hand to apologize, you really mean it. But you don't feel badly enough to give away the point.

What the %$#& was that winners
These are shots wherein you take a wild, half-blind swipe at the
ball and hit it for a winner. Typically, it's a swinging volley from
near the baseline or a backhand overhead that you just flail at,
yet the ball somehow finds a tiny piece of the court. Instead of
holding up your racket to apologize, you shrug your shoulders
and hold your palms out as if to say, "I don't know what the
%$#& that was either."

Totally embarrassing winners
There are two candidates here.
1) The first is when you go back for a deep lob intending to
   nail the overhead, but miss the ball completely. However,
   the ball lands just out and your partner, a sarcastic SOB
   says, "Good eye."

2) The second is when you get a short lob that you want to kill,
   but at the last second you look down, drop your racket-
   head and catch the ball on the top of the frame. It barely
   goes over the net then dies before your opponents can reach
   it. Your partner, yet another smartass, says, "Nice touch."

There's no sense in even raising your racket to apologize
for such shots. Just delete them from your memory bank as if
they never happened. However, you might want to find more
sympathetic partners.

Inside-the-court aces
These are serves you hit so weakly they bounce twice before
reaching the receiver. As if this weren't bad enough, there are
some players who actually take credit for an ace. It should be
noted that there are players who can intentionally hit backspin
on a serve. A few are so good at it that you have to cover the
serve like a drop shot.

Now for the mistakes…

Drop shots (or drop volleys) that land well beyond the service line

Pretty self-explanatory. More often than not, you're going to eat these.

Extreme topspin forehands that hit the top of the frame and end up in a tree

At many clubs you get a do-over if you nail a squirrel.

Shots that land in another court

Fortunately, you can only lose one point on a shot no matter how bad it is.

Serves that hit your partner

Normally, this is a negative statistic, but it becomes a positive one if your partner is a world-class jackass.

Short lobs that put your partner in the hospital

(See above.)

Overheads that don't even reach the net

The worst part about these shots is that everyone on the court has time to turn and watch you butcher them.

Urban Tennis
Warning: Political incorrectness ahead

Anyone who has played tennis on the public courts of a large city knows they present obstacles and challenges not seen in country club venues. Therefore, urban tennis players have devised their own on-court rules and safety precautions to deal with the metropolitan environment. They include the following:

Prior to the match you should…

- Check to see which gang controls the local turf so you'll be certain not to wear a rival gang's colors.

The urban environment presents unique challenges for tennis players.

- Make sure your car radio is not pre-set to country music stations.

- Take along some dollar bills for the times when a wino grabs one of your tennis balls and holds it for ransom.

- Also, bring extra cash to pay the "neighborhood watch" representative for "safeguarding" your tennis bag.

During the match you can play a let if...

- You miss a shot while trying to sidestep a hypodermic needle.

- A gunfight breaks out as you're hitting your serve.

- A SWAT team raids an adjacent court.

- You get mugged while going back for a deep lob.

- A crackhead wanders onto your court.

It's Not Just a Game
It's a commitment

If you are an avid, long-time tennis player, your relationship to the game is apt to be more of a lifetime commitment than a recreational diversion. Indeed, the process of developing your game is much like the process of choosing a life partner. For example, the beginning phase of tennis is akin to the first awkward dates with a new love interest. You fumble about as you try to find a comfort level but, because of your unfamiliarity, it doesn't come easily. Nevertheless, you are aware that strong feelings have been aroused in you and you want to pursue the relationship.

As you become increasingly adept, your feelings intensify and you enter the courtship stage. Now you are consumed by the fiery passion of young love and you can't get enough of the game. You play two, three, even four hours a day when you can.

Soon you transition to the engagement phase and affirm your love by purchasing $250 racket.

Then comes the marriage and for the first few years all goes well. Eventually, however, your game reaches a plateau and the ardor and excitement begin to fade. You sink into the day-to-day monotony of playing at the same level, and you begin to question your lifetime commitment.

Finally, you decide you need a break from the game; if not a complete split, at least a trial separation. So you put away your tennis equipment and begin flirting with new, hot games. You go through a phase of tawdry liaisons with other racket sports— morning trysts with squash, nooners of racketball and torrid nights of table tennis. However, these dalliances leave you empty and unfulfilled, for they are purely physical, all lust and no love.

Then one day you drive by your tennis club and those old feelings well up in you. So you fetch your tennis gear and arrange a few hitting sessions. As you walk on the court, you know in your heart you've returned home, and you realize that this is the sport you want to grow old with. But this time, with the wisdom of experience, you accept the game on its own terms, happy to be out there, not worrying about how you play.

From now on, you decide, you'll live by the old adage that any day of tennis is a good day… unless you play lousy and lose to your arch nemesis. Even old adages have their limits.

The International Tennis Hall of Fame (ITHF)

If you love the game, you'll love the Hall of Fame. Housed in the historic Newport Casino, the museum area is relatively compact but contains virtually the entire history of tennis, from the earliest days to the most recent Grand Slam. You can learn enough history in just a few hours to annoy your tennis friends for months.

The ITHF is located in the elegant city of Newport, Rhode Island, and is a throwback to the gilded age of America. Indeed, as you stroll the stately grounds adjacent to the grass courts, you half expect Gatsby and Daisy to come bounding out of the clubhouse for a rousing match with Nick and Jordan.

After touring the ITHF, the next must-see are the Newport mansions, just to give you an idea of how much money you don't have. While these grand homes have names such as The Breakers, The Elms and Marble House, they were mere cottages for the super-rich of the time. A place where they could "summer" in the parlance of the wealthy. You know you have serious money when your second home has a name and you use "summer" as a verb.

Like the city itself, the ITHF is a class act, one that every ardent tennis player should catch.

Greatest Tennis Quote Ever
Even if it might not have been true

The occasion was the Grand Prix Masters Tennis Tournament held in New York City's Madison Square Garden in mid-January of 1980. Vitas Gerulaitis was playing Jimmy Connors, a man who had defeated him sixteen times in a row. After Gerulaitis won the match he was asked by the on-court commentator why he was finally able to beat Connors after so many consecutive losses. A grinning Vitas responded, "Because nobody beats Vitas Gerulaitis seventeen times in a row."

Many people erroneously believe that Gerulaitis was referring to Bjorn Borg, which is not unreasonable since Vitas had an even longer losing streak against the Swede. Then again, maybe he didn't. The ATP lists the head-to-head record as 16-0, while other sources indicate it may have been as high as 20-0. Whatever the record, Gerulaitis' quote is widely considered the most famous in tennis history and one of the most famous in all of sports.

Gerulaitis had a fine career, winning one Grand Slam and making it to the finals of two others. Sadly, he is not enshrined in the International Tennis Hall of Fame, even though many people think he should be, if not for his career then for his quote. Even more sadly, he died at the age of forty from carbon monoxide poisoning due to a faulty gas heater.

However, long after many of his more celebrated contemporaries are remembered only by their names in a record book or plaques on a wall, Vitas and his quote will live on in tennis lore. Everyone loves a guy who can laugh at himself so endearingly.

Player Quotes

"The trouble with me is that every match I play against five opponents: umpire, crowd, ball boys, court and myself."
Goran Ivanisevic, explaining his inconsistency

"I hope so. Otherwise, I'd feel lonely."
Marat Safin, on being asked if he had multiple personalities

"My tennis pro told me that if I paid a little more for better strings they would last longer. I told him that at my age I don't even buy green bananas."
A super-senior tennis player

"I don't think anyone ever feared him in the locker room."
Todd Martin, on being asked if he thought Pete Sampras had finally lost the fear factor in the locker room

"I played really well so I'd like to thank myself."
Dmitry Tursunov at an awards presentation ceremony

"I guess I made a lot of mistakes."
Venus Williams, on why her unforced error count was so high

"How to shake hands."
Bettina Bunge, on what she had learned from a series of rapid defeats to Martina Navratilova

"Now I like it again."
Roger Federer, on his rivalry with Rafael Nadal after beating the Spaniard in the Wimbledon final for the first time in five meetings

"I wore that to a sixth-grade dance."
Robby Ginepri, on Vince Spadea's outfit in Miami

Chapter IV

Pros and Cons
(Rants, raves, records and rivalries)

There are many tennis fans who are not greatly enamored of the modern professional game. The reason is that raw power has almost completely driven guile, finesse and touch off the court. Granted, the athleticism of the players has increased significantly, but at the expense of variety and point construction. With rare exceptions, singles matches have become baseline (or serving) slugfests, while tactics such as serve/volley and chip/charge have gone the way of rotary phones and eight-track tapes.

(Which, incidentally, I had by the boxful when they first came out because I decided they were the ultimate in music storage technology. *Nothing will ever top this,* I thought as I was adjusting my TV antenna so I could get all four channels, none of which I really wanted to watch. We've come a long way since then. I can now get over a thousand channels that I don't want to watch. Isn't it amazing how so many skilled and talented show biz people can make so many awful movies?) But I digress.

As long as the subject is complaining about pro tennis, there are a few others items to throw in the mix.

The Three (or four) Ball Shuffle

This happens when the server gets three or four balls from the ball kid, looks at them briefly, keeps two and tosses the others back as if to say, "Being a highly skilled professional I can look at these balls for about a micro-second and instantly identify the ones that have naps which are one thousandth of an inch smaller and will therefore fly through the air .04% faster."

Pre-serve ball-checking has gotten completely out of hand.

Baloney. They change balls after the first seven games, then each nine games after that. Other than the occasional fluffy one, they're essentially the same.

What I think happened is that one pro started doing this, probably for a lark, and the others decided they better do it too lest they appear to be out of the loop. It's a pointless sideshow and impresses no one.

Toweling Off After Every Point

Isn't it enough that the ball kids have to scoop up the balls, scamper off the court, then deliver them to the right location? Do they have to be towel-bearers, too? God forbid professional tennis players should have to start a point with even a drop of perspiration on their faces. And just how sweaty do they get after a two-second rally? It's not like they're playing in a sauna. What's next, sponge baths on the changeovers? Sometimes I think the men should change their organization's name to the ATW—the Association of Tennis Weenies.

Pre-serve Rituals

Players who are incessantly bouncing the ball, sweeping their hair, adjusting their headbands and tugging at their shorts before they serve have become very tiresome to the audience. After you watch them for a while you want to scream, "For God's sakes, you're not launching a nuclear missile; you're serving a tennis ball. Hit the damn thing already."

Unsound Effects

For the three-ball shuffle and excessive toweling, men are the worst offenders. However, when it comes to adding a sound track to the game, women are the clear winners. Men just use the basic grunt with a few individual variations, whereas women have added a whole repertoire of irritating noises including shrieking, hooting and yelping in addition to grunting. Some women's matches sound more like auditions for a porno flick than athletic contests. (At least, what I *imagine* a porno flick sounds like.)

There's not much officials can do about it but, thankfully, we all have "mute" buttons. Of course, you miss the commentary, but if you're an experienced player you know what they're going to say most of the time.

One can only hope that the tennis powers are squelching this practice at the junior level. Otherwise, the only people watching women's matches in the future will be lecherous males fantasizing about all that screaming, but under very different circumstances.

Now for some good things…

The Shot Spot Review

Best technical innovation ever. It is particularly dramatic when the ball is very close to the line on a big point. The image zooms in closer and closer, the crowd starts its rhythmic clapping, until… it's in (or out) by a millimeter. The crowd likes it, the players like it and the chair umpires, those poor souls who, God only knows why, submit themselves to public abuse and ridicule, absolutely love it.

Of course, some players take advantage of the system, particularly when they are challenging an "out" call on one of their shots. The rule says that the challenge must be done in a timely manner. Timely does not mean checking the mark, looking over at the friend's box, querying the umpire and asking the crowd. The rule should be the same as the three-second rule for dropping food on the floor. If you don't do it within the allotted time, you've missed your chance. (Note: The three-second rule for food on the floor is a really bad idea. It's the same as eating something off the bottom of your shoe. Who would do that?)

The Tie-breaker

Although it's been around since 1965, the tie-breaker remains one of the best ideas in the history of tennis. If not for the tie-breaker, players could get into the kind of ridiculous scenario I once saw in an over-the-top tennis movie. The premise is totally unbelievable but it makes for a pretty good story so here's a recap.

There were these two pros named Johnny and Nicky, who were playing in the first round of Wimbledon. They were tied at two sets apiece when play was suspended for darkness. They began the fifth set the following day, and, since Wimbledon doesn't employ tie-breakers in the final set, they continued past six-all. They were big guys with big serves so both were holding easily, and the score soon reached twenty-all. At this point avid tennis fans all over the world began tuning to radio Wimbledon or surfing to websites that relayed the score.

They continued holding serve and eventually reached thirty-all. By this time casual tennis fans, even non-tennis fans, were following the match. On and on they played until the score reached forty-all. Now you must be thinking, *FORTY-ALL? How gullible do they think we are? That's ridiculous!* Indeed it is, but Hollywood movies always stretch the bonds of credibility.

Nevertheless, they played on reaching a score of fifty-all, at which point the scoreboard failed and had to be reset to 0 - 0. By this time the entire world was transfixed—from Murmansk to Melbourne, from mud huts to mansions, from the crème de la crème to the dregs of society. Wars and plans for war were temporarily halted and for a few golden hours there was world peace. Historians even named this era "Pax Wimbledon." When the score got to fifty-nine apiece the match was suspended due to darkness.

Overnight, conspiracy theories began popping up on the Internet. One theory alleged that the two players prearranged the match so they could be in the record books. Another claimed that the Illuminati and Trilateral Commission staged it as a diversion so they could take over the world's money supply. (Which is absurd since they have already done that… according to some radio talk show hosts.)

In playgrounds throughout England small children were singing nursery rhymes about the match.

> Johnny and Nicky
> Got into a sticky
> They played forever
> 'Cause no tie-breaker
> So on they played
> 'Til John nearly died
> And all the tennis world
> Went for a ride

Play resumed the next day until Johnny finally broke serve to win by a score of 70 - 68. The records set by the match are too numerous, not to mention too outrageous, to list. One example is the total number of aces, 216 (113 by Johnny and 103 by Nicky). Of course, the match is a complete fabrication and could never happen in real life, but it can still serve as an object lesson to Grand Slam officials who refuse to opt for a fifth set tie-breaker.

Dubious Records

Researching and categorizing tennis records can drive you nuts because of all the criteria and conditions involved. There are men and women, singles and doubles, multiple surfaces,

Grand Slam vs. regular tourneys, single season vs. career records, and so on. It's impossible to factor in all the variables and still come up with an objective rating standard, although tennis commentators try to do that all the time.

For example, are Roger Federer's 23 straight Grand Slam semi-final appearances more impressive than Margaret Smith Court's 62 Major titles, singles, doubles and mixed doubles combined? Are Rod Laver's two calendar Grand Slams (albeit one prior to the Open Era) worth more than Steffi Graf's 22 Grand Slam titles, which includes winning all four Majors at least four times and a Golden Slam, i.e., the calendar Grand Slam plus Olympic gold? Who's to say? So here are some records that stand on their own:

Most fined top-tier players for code violations
Women: Serena Williams
Men: John McEnroe

No surprises here. Quite often, the passion, intensity and arrogance of elite athletes erupt into very bad behavior when things go south for them. As long as they're successful in major tournaments they're referred to as temperamental geniuses. Once they stop winning they become obnoxious crybabies. Also, the entire world has easy access to captured video so their worst moments will be on display forever. Kind of makes you glad you're not a superstar tennis player, doesn't it? (Me neither.)

Most double faults in a singles match at a major tournament
Women: 31, by Anna Kournikova at the Australian Open, including two when she held match points. Somehow, she still won the match, which proves the old adage, "If you're cute enough you can get away with damn near anything." The crowd, however, was not amused.
Men: Who cares?

Most unforced errors in a singles match at a major tournament
  Women: 103, by Daniela Hantuchova, at the French Open.
  Men: 112, by Yevgeny Kafelnikov, also at the French Open.
  Kafelnikov won while Hantuchova lost, which tends to contradict the cuteness adage.

Most painful looking shot
  (Warning: Graphic description of bodily injury)
  Women: Kim Clijsters
  Men: Novak Djokovic
  The shot is the full-split forehand, originated by Clijsters and carried forward by Djokovic. It's painful to watch at normal camera speeds, but when you see it in slow-motion replay you can almost feel your groin muscles being ripped apart, as if evil giants were playing make-a-wish with your legs.

Most rackets smashed
  Women: This is primarily a testosterone-induced activity.
  Men: Mention the name Marat Safin to serious tennis fans and racket-smashing immediately comes to mind. There are no official numbers for this category but conservative estimates put Safin's career total at over 700 and his single season record at around 100. However, for sheer intensity of racket-smashing, the relatively composed Marcos Baghdatis takes the prize. At the 2012 Australian Open Marcos destroyed four of his rackets in less than 60 seconds.

  No discussion of racket smashing, or quirkiness in general, would be complete without mentioning Goran Ivanisevic, who, at a tournament in England, smashed *all* his rackets and defaulted the match. (Note: Ivanisevic is also tied with Safin for shorts-dropping in front of a sizeable crowd. The current score is one-all, at least as far as official records go.)

An honorable mention goes to Mikhail Youzhny who tried to smash a racket against his head at a tournament in Miami, Florida. The racket escaped unscathed but Youzhny's head didn't fare as well. Fortunately, he was not a senior citizen at the time or he would have been charged with "abuse of the elderly," a serious crime in Florida.

Worst incident ever at a professional match

This happened to Monica Seles but the perpetrator was male. The facts are straightforward and well-known. On April 30, 1993, a man named Gunter Parche rushed out of the stands at a tournament in Hamburg, Germany and stabbed Ms. Seles in the back. Parche was arrested and eventually sentenced to a long prison term for assault with a deadly weapon. At least, that's what *should* have happened, right?

What did happen is that the guy was given a two-year suspended sentence on the basis that he was too "mentally disturbed" to understand the grievous nature of his act. However, he wasn't too disturbed to figure out how to carry out the act, nor to understand he was knocking Seles out of the game because she had supplanted Steffi Graf as the top women's player.

Can you imagine what the consequences would have been if a non-German assaulted a German tennis star? He wouldn't just be thrown *in* jail, he'd be planted *under* the jail. "German justice" is the ultimate oxymoron.

Most brutal (but funny) characterization of a pro

Bud Collins, referring to Martina Navratilova as "the Great Wide Hope." When Martina defected to the US in 1975 she discovered America's two greatest assets, freedom and food. For a time she overindulged in both, then did a complete turnaround and became one of the fittest players in the history of the game.

Strangest player

German pro Karsten Braasch. First off, Braasch wore goggle-glasses that made him look more like an arc-welder than a tennis player. Second, he had a service motion right out of the *Twilight Zone*. Third, he was known to smoke cigarettes during the changeovers. Finally, while Braasch achieved a career-high singles ranking of 38, his most notable victories were over Venus and Serena Williams in exhibition matches, although Serena was only 17 at the time.

Best impressionist

Ivan Lendl, hands down. Most tennis fans would be surprised to learn that Lendl is a master of this art and can do a wide range of delightful impressions including...

- The Sphinx
- A cadaver
- Dried fruit
- Wood
- Bill Belichick (Head Coach of the NFL's New England Patriots, who's about as expressive as... Ivan Lendl)

Best carbohydrate reference

Eddie Dibbs and Harold Solomon for using the word "bagel" to refer to a love set. Utilized as both a noun and a verb (e.g., She got bageled.), it has become an established part of the tennis lexicon. An honorable mention goes to whoever applied the word "breadstick" to refer to a 6-1 set.

Consecutive days locking one's keys in one's car by a non-professional tennis player

Women: None that come to mind.

Men: Three, but I'd rather not say by whom.

One record that no one wants to break is…

The point from hell

The longest point ever played in a professional match occurred on Sept. 24, 1984, when Vicki Nelson and Jean Hepner engaged in a 29-minute, 643-shot rally during the first round of a Virginia Slim's tournament in Richmond, Virginia. The reason we know the shot count is that a courtside reporter from *The Richmond Times-Dispatch* had the foresight to keep track of the strokes.

During that point the following events happened:

- Approximately 5,200 babies were born
- Approximately 2,900 people died
- People in Indiana flushed their toilets over half a million times

That last statistic is rather obscure but it could be interesting to some Indiana tennis players. After all, other than the Colts, the car race and the fact that the official state rock is limestone, there's just not much going on there.

The Rivalry…
that launched a thousand metaphors

Between 1973 and 1988, Chris Evert and Martina Navratilova played each other a total of 80 times. The following is a recap of their meetings.

- All finals: Navratilova 36–25
- Grand Slam matches: Navratilova 14–8
- Grand Slam finals: Navratilova 10–4
- Grand Slam semifinals: Tied 4–4
- Non-Grand Slam finals: Tied 19–19
- Three-set matches: Evert 16–14

In terms of big match rivalries, nothing in tennis even comes close. For example, Bjorn Borg and Jimmy Connors played each other 30 times—eight of those matches were in Major tournaments including five Grand Slam finals. Rod Laver and Ken Rosewall played each other over 140 times, but only twice in Grand Slam finals.

The contrasting styles and on court personas of Evert and Navratilova fairly scream out for metaphorical comparisons, so here goes.

- One is a fiery Amazon
  The other an icy assassin

- One is an onrushing tsunami
  The other an impregnable barricade

- One wears her emotions on her sleeve
  The other keeps her emotions in a sleeve

- One is a consummate athlete
  The other a master tactician

- One is an attacking jungle cat
  The other an expert lion-tamer

- One has the flair of a riverboat gambler
  The other the calmness of a cloistered nun

- One is a ballistic missile
  The other a laser deterrent

- One is a lefty
  The other a righty

- One is out of metaphors
  The other is too

You Bet

Like most human endeavors, gambling on professional tennis has its good points and bad points. These are shown below:

<u>**Good points**</u>

1) You can win money.

2) It makes the matches more exciting.

3) You get to test your tennis knowledge.

4) If you're good, you can quit your job. If not, you'll work harder.

5) You learn new math skills such as calculating and applying probabilities.

6) It saves you from deciding what to do with your discretionary income.

7) You meet interesting people when you start going to all those gambling addiction rehab meetings.

<u>**Bad points**</u>

1) You can lose money.

I think most tennis fans would agree that some pro matches can be pretty boring. However, when you put down a sizeable bet you will be riveted by almost every point, assuming the match is at all competitive. Furthermore, as the old joke goes, you can make a small fortune... if you start with a large fortune.

Before venturing into the world of gambling here's a quick quiz to see if you're really ready. Let's say you're tossing a "fair coin," i.e., a coin that has an equal probability of coming up head or tails. Here are the questions.

What is the probability of tossing four heads in a row?

If you toss four heads in a row, what is the probability that the next toss will be heads?

The answers? If you don't know off the top of your head, you shouldn't be gambling.

The Need for Speed

One of the big attractions at a pro tennis match is the service speed display. Whenever someone cracks a big one people always look at the display, sometimes before the point is over. In fact, you can often tell the speed range of a serve from the crowd reaction. Here are some examples. (We'll use men's first serve numbers because they are, no offense, bigger than the women's.)

Speed Range*	Crowd Reaction
< 120 mph	General derision. Lots of snickering and mockery.
120 - 125 mph	Very little reaction except a few shoulder shrugs and eye-rolls, as if to say, "That all you got?"
126 - 130 mph	A few scattered "oohs." Polite applause.
131 - 135 mph	Numerous "oohs" and "aahs." Vigorous applause.
136 - 140 mph	Vociferous shouting, hooting and whistling. A few people rise and clap.
141 - 145 mph	Great excitement and shouts of approval. Half the audience stands and cheers.
146 - 150 mph	People leap out of their seats screaming, "WOW!" and "YES!"
> 150 mph	Women swoon; men wail and cry. Cell phones explode.

*Multiply by 1.61 to get kph.

Undoubtedly, there are many questions racing though your mind, including those below.

Q: Where the hell are my spare car keys?

A: Let's confine our questions to serving speeds, shall we?

Q: Where is the ball speed measured?

A: Just after the point of impact at its maximum velocity.

Q: Can you show the equations that describe the motion of the ball, and solve them for a serve with an initial velocity of 132 mph, a tailwind of 7 mph, at an altitude of 1,756 feet and a temperature of 76° F?

A: No.

Q: Okay then, can you summarize what happens to the ball in flight?

A: According to the experts, there are three main forces acting on the ball after it is struck.

1) Air resistance, which slows the ball considerably, although the magnitude depends on the wind speed and direction.

2) Gravity, which adds a small, downward component to the ball's velocity.

3) Hitting the ground, which also slows the ball significantly.

Q: What is the ball speed when it gets to the receiver?

A: The consensus is about 40 - 50% of the initial speed.

Q: How long does it take for a serve of 130 mph to get to the receiver?

A: As a first approximation, let's assume the average speed is half the initial speed plus the final speed. Let's also assume the receiver is seven feet behind the baseline. For a serve hit at 130 mph the average speed would be about 95 mph or 140 feet/sec. To cover the 85 feet between server and receiver, neglecting the vertical component, would take about 0.60 seconds.

Q: How accurate are the measurements?

A: Compared to Olympic timekeeping not very accurate, but since they're for entertainment purposes it doesn't really matter. Recent tests among the leading speed systems indicate that differences average about 3%, but in some tests they were as high as 10%.

Q: What's the fastest serve ever measured in a sanctioned pro match?

A: 156 mph (251 kph) by Croatian Ivo Karlovic in a Davis Cup match.

Q: Still no help with the car keys?

A: No, other than to suggest you make three sets—one to use, one to store and one to lose.

The Egg Team

Running the gamut from A to Z—Amanmuradova to Zakopalova—the "ova" ladies (a.k.a., the Egg Team) have become a dominant presence in women's professional tennis. As of this writing (March 2013), there were 19 "ovas" in the top 100 of the WTA rankings, including two in the top ten.

Egg Team members come in a variety of styles, from sunny-side-up golden girls such as Maria Sharapova, to hard-boiled grinders like Dominika Cibulkova and, finally, to the ovum emeritus, the Eggs Benedict of the team, Martina Navratilova. (Note: "Over easy" is not one of the categories.)

With the ever-increasing popularity of tennis in Russia and Eastern Europe, this trend is expected to continue for decades. The only question is why executives in the egg industry aren't scrambling to become major sponsors of the women's tour. Their brains must be fried. (Sorry about that, but once you get trapped in egg terminology, you end up in a real pickle and it's the devil to get out of it.)

The "ova ladies" are dominating women's tennis.

Vitamin D Roulette

There is evidence to suggest that Vitamin D levels in the blood are an important factor in preventing certain types of organ cancers; and the best way to get Vitamin D is through sun exposure. However, there is also evidence to suggest that excessive solar radiation is a major cause of skin cancer.

So what's a pro (or non-pro) tennis player, who spends countless hours in the sun, to do? That depends on your latitude. If you're in southern Florida in the summer, go heavy on the sunscreen. If you're in northern Minnesota in the winter, get the hell out.

GOATs and Zombies

According to the basic rules of decorum, there are three topics that should never be discussed in polite company: religion, politics and GOATs. Not the barnyard animals, the **G**reatest **O**f **A**ll **T**ime tennis players. Of these three topics, the most bitterly contentious is the GOAT issue. In fact, the GOAT issue has been discussed so often and so fervently that it has become, in modern parlance, a "zombie topic." Which means it has been beaten to death by hordes of over-zealous tennis fans, yet it keeps coming back to life.

Unlike an actual zombie (well, an actual movie zombie), which can be exterminated by a variety of means, the GOAT debate cannot be killed off. Someday, when you're really bored and need a mindless activity to keep you occupied, go to a tennis message board and start a GOAT debate. However, you should be prepared for a mud-slinging contest regardless of how reasonable you try to be. There are lots of jerks on the web and tennis sites have their share.

To help you out, there are two tables below which contain significant stats for the top-ranked men and women.

Men's Statistics

	Grand Slam Titles	Singles Match Record	Weeks at No. 1
Roger Federer*	Aus: 4 French: 1 Wimby: 7 USO: 5 **Total: 17**	Titles: 76 W-L: 878-198 (81.6%)	302
Rod Laver	Aus: 3 French: 2 Wimby: 4 USO: 2 **Total: 11 (5 in Open Era)**	Titles: 41 (Open Era only) W-L: 411-107 (79.3%) (Open Era only)	N/A
Pete Sampras	Aus: 2 French: 0 Wimby: 7 USO: 5 **Total: 14**	Titles: 64 W-L: 762-222 (77.4%)	286
Bjorn Borg	Aus: 0 French: 6 Wimby: 5 USO: 0 **Total: 11**	Titles: 64 W-L: 608-127 (82.7%)	109
Rafael Nadal*	Aus: 1 French: 7 Wimby: 2 USO: 1 **Total: 11**	Titles: 50 W-L: 583-122 (82.7%)	102

*Stats for Roger and Rafa are as of 3/1/2013.

The wild card on the list is Laver because he won six of his eleven Grand Slams before the Open Era. On the flip side, he lost five years in the heart of his career when pros couldn't compete in the Grand Slams.

Women's Statistics

	Grand Slam Titles	Singles Match Record	Weeks at No. 1
Martina Navratilova	Aus: 3 French: 2 Wimby: 9 USO: 4 **Total: 18**	Titles: 167 W-L: 1,442-219 (86.8%)	332
Steffi Graf	Aus: 4 French: 6 Wimby: 7 USO: 5 **Total: 22**	Titles: 107 W-L: 902-155 (88.7%)	377
Chris Evert	Aus: 2 French: 7 Wimby: 3 USO: 6 **Total: 18**	Titles: 157 W-L: 1,309-145 (90.7%)	260
Margaret Court	Aus: 11 French: 5 Wimby: 3 USO: 5 **Total: 24** **(11 in Open Era)**	Titles: 192 (92 in Open era) W-L: 1,117-106 (91.7%)	N/A
Serena Williams*	Aus: 5 French: 1 Wimby: 5 USO: 4 **Total: 15**	Titles: 47 W-L: 558-108 (84.0%)	123
Billie Jean King	Aus: 1 French: 1 Wimby: 6 USO: 4 **Total: 12** **(9 in Open Era)**	Titles: 129 (84 in Open era) W-L: 695-155 (81.8%)	N/A

*Stats for Serena are as of 3/1/2013.

(Personally, I think Graf and Navratilova should be co-number ones because of Martina's doubles record.)

The wild card on the list is Margaret Court who won the majority of her titles prior to the Open Era. However, she won 24 Grand Slam singles titles and 38 combined Grand Slam titles in doubles and mixed, so you just can't keep her off.

Where Does the Pro Game Go From Here?

If you were to watch a series of films and videos that depict the history of tennis, assuming you had a lot of free time on your hands, you would see a host of dramatic changes. Tennis has gone from a genteel game of pit-a-pat to the modern game of full-on ball-bashing and frenzied court-dashing. The equipment has progressed from modest-sized wood rackets with natural gut to high-tech howitzers with synthetic strings that suit all styles of play.

It does seem curious that animal intestines would become a popular material for racket strings. I suppose that when the first person who played with gut started winning consistently, everyone had to try it. Let's face it, a lot of serious tennis players would figure out a way to use their own intestines if they thought it would make a significant improvement in their games.

One can only wonder where the sport goes from here. Is the unrelenting pursuit of power a pendulum that will eventually swing the other way or a runaway train that will continue gathering speed? The latter seems more likely. It's hard to imagine tennis equipment companies marketing rackets that are less powerful or strings that are less responsive.

Furthermore, the combination of enormous power and the high-kicking topspin required to keep the ball in the court favors taller players more and more. The odds are stacked against male players shorter that six feet or female players shorter than five

Like basketball, tennis favors the taller player.

feet eight inches winning a Grand Slam tournament. Pro tennis has become a sport for taller players and this trend can only get worse, or better, depending on your vantage point.

So what's the solution? Who knows? You can teach a kid how to hit a great forehand; you can't teach him how to be tall.

Of course, you can always go on the Internet and search for websites on how to grow taller. If you do you'll find information that is…

1) Useless: Have tall parents.

2) Dangerous: How to build and use a stretch rack. (Wasn't this a torture device at one time?)

3) Questionable: Various programs with names such as, *Growing Taller for Idiots.* I have no idea if such programs actually work, but I think people should be skeptical about dealing with companies whose tacit slogan is "Only idiots buy our products."

The only other option, for the men anyway, is to be a Croatian. Check out the height of some top Croatian tennis players, past and present.

Goran Ivanisevic: 6 ft 4 in (1.93 m)
Ivan Ljubicic: 6 ft 4 in (1.93 m)
Marin Cilic: 6 ft 6 in (1.98 m)
Ivo Karlovic:, 6 ft 10 in (2.08 m)
Mario Ancic: 6 ft 5 in (1.95 m)

If I were an aspiring young player with a family trait of shortness, I'd consider applying for Croatian citizenship. If that weren't feasible I'd at least add an "ic" to the end of my last name. It's worth a shot.

Commentator Quotes

"Henman should leave here with his head hung high."
Jonathan Overend

"McEnroe has got to sit down and work out where he stands."
Fred Perry

"The unstoppable juggernaut of women's tennis has just been run over by a Lori."
The Sun, on Steffi Graf's first round loss to Lori McNeil at Wimbledon

"Obviously, like Wembley is synonymous with tennis, snooker is synonymous with Sheffield."
Richard Caborn, British Minister for Sport

"Federer is just the third person ever to achieve this impossible feat."
BBC Radio

"She could swing from arrogance to panic with nothing in between."
Ted Tinling (British tennis apparel designer) on Martina Navratilova

"Strangely enough, Kathy Jordan is getting to the net first, which she always does."
Fred Perry

"She comes from a tennis playing family. Her father's a dentist."
BBC radio

Chapter V

Court Jesters
(Characters we meet between the alleys)

One of the most engaging aspects of a sport like tennis is that you meet a host of intriguing characters along the way, many of whom have very creative styles of play. Some are entertaining, some are exasperating and some are just plain goofy. Taken together they make up a fascinating collection.

The "Don't ask or they'll tell" Mugs

You stroll into your tennis club and greet people with the standard, "Hey, how ya doin'?"

They respond with, "Fine, and you?"

Then you say, "Fine, thanks."

This goes on until you encounter one of the "Don't ask or they'll tell" mugs. Apparently, these people think that "How ya doin'?" is a question not a greeting because they tell you how they're doing, usually in graphic detail. For example, they'll say, "Of course, you know about the shoulder issue I've had for the past nine years. (And you do know because they've mentioned it every time you've seen them for the past nine years.) It's gotten a lot worse. My orthopedist told me that if I keep playing tennis my arm will literally fall off.

"And I'm sure you heard that I injured my knee going back for a deep lob. I'll get back to that in a minute, but my worst problem is that I had such a severe case of the flu that I had to be hospitalized. The doctors said I had the highest fever they'd ever seen in a person who lived. In fact, it fried the part of my brain that controls backhand volleys so I can't hit those anymore. But back to my knee..."

You finally interrupt and say, "Listen, this is really fascinating. Why don't you fax me your entire medical history so I can study it in detail when I have more time."

But do they get the hint? Hell, no. They whip out their cell phones and say, "Sure. What's your fax number?"

The Terminators

These are the players who end most of the points one way or the other. They operate on a two-tiered system.

Plan A) Hit it hard

Plan B) Hit it harder

If neither of those options is working, get out of the way because the next shot is going through you or through the back fence.

Their objective is not necessarily to win the match, but to be the hardest hitter out there. As their opponent your job is simply to get the ball back in the court if you can so the Terminators can kill it. Furthermore, it doesn't matter what kind of shot you hit them. They can botch an easy shot just as easily as they can hit a winner off a tough one, more easily for that matter.

When they do hit winners they're pretty spectacular— almost as spectacular as their errors, which have been known to warp the back fence or knock down a net-post. The best strategy against a Terminator is to hit the ball deep with very little pace, then stand aside. They'll miss at least one out of two and, quite often, injure themselves in the process. Unfortunately, they'll be back.

The Coachmasters

These folks are usually seniors who play only doubles. Their skills and mobility are limited, but their tennis knowledge, in their minds at least, is virtually infinite. When you partner with

Coachmasters they are going to share their knowledge with you whether you want them to or not. They will give you detailed instructions on where to stand, where to move and how to hit the ball. They are particularly prone to do this when they are serving, primarily to compensate for their lack of court coverage. They will give you meticulous directions such as move to your left exactly nine and a half inches at an angle of 37 degrees to the center service line.

Furthermore, Coachmasters can do no wrong. If a Coachmaster hits a short lob that nearly gets you killed, he will spend the next three minutes telling you what you did wrong leading up to the incident.

Quite often, a Coachmaster's advice can lead to comical situations. I recall a match wherein the Coachmaster came in for a volley and was pulled into the alley. He hit a weak crosscourt volley and, unable to recover, left a gaping hole up the middle. The opponent hit a winner through the hole, whereupon the Coachmaster screamed at his partner. "You're supposed to cover the middle when I get pulled wide!"

A couple of points later the same thing happened. This time the Coachmaster's partner moved to the middle leaving the alley wide open, so the opponent hit an easy winner down the line. Whereupon the Coachmaster again berated his partner. "You're supposed to cover the alley!"

To which his partner responded, "You just told me to cover the middle! Make up your freakin' mind!"

If you get trapped as a Coachmaster's partner you have several options, but first you have to decide whether you want to win the match or irritate the SOB. If it's the latter, then the first time he tells you what you did wrong, you say to him, "Shut the #%&@ up or I'll (insert your favorite tennis threat here).” Or, “I’ll play any way I damn well please. If you don’t like it you can go to (insert your favorite netherworld location here).” These sorts of comments do not foster team unity and will probably cost you the match.

If you don’t care, that’s fine, but if you do your options are limited. When he starts giving you instructions, you just have to stand there and take it. However, you can express your anger in a non-verbal way. The next time you serve, nail him in the back with your first delivery. When he turns around to complain, you say, “Gee, I’m sorry, but you were standing right in my line of fire. How about moving to your left exactly nine and a half inches at an angle of 37 degrees to the center service line.”

The Geeks

If you’re like most tennis players you usually don’t keep a cyanide pill embedded in your mouth. However, if you ever get cornered by a tennis geek you might wish you had one, just to give yourself a viable means of bailing out.

The geeks always seem to come at you during your most vulnerable moments, such as when you’re at a tennis function and you don’t know anybody. They can sense you’re desperate for conversation so they pounce on you like a vulture on roadkill. They introduce themselves, and, before you can even respond, they ask, “Do you know who won the US Open in 1992?”

Caught off guard, you stumble for an answer and finally say, “Um… Boris Becker?”

“Nope, nope, you’re wrong,” they say (which they love doing). “It was Stefan Edberg over Pete Sampras 3-6, 6-4, 7-6, 6-2.” Then, without your asking or showing the slightest bit of interest, they give you the match details and stats, complete with replays of the biggest points, ad in, ad out, ad nauseum.

At this point, many thoughts are racing through your mind, such as...

Why would anyone know all this?

How can I get away from this guy?

Where the hell is my cyanide pill?

(Note: There is an organization known as The Hemlock Society that provides information for people who want to hasten their ends, but it's doubtful they make emergency calls.)

The Non-Stop Commentators
Babbling as an art form

These are the people, commonly referred to as babblers, who talk incessantly throughout a tennis match. However, male and female babblers tend to do so differently. Male babblers usually confine their discussion to the match being played, providing a running commentary after each point. That wouldn't be so bad except they never say anything interesting or entertaining. They just say things like, "He missed the overhead because the sun was in his eyes." Or, "That was in, but it would have been out if he'd hit it harder." It's like color commentary without the color.

Female babblers are more wide-ranging in their ramblings and provide stream-of-consciousness commentary such as, "Oh, Linda, that was such a good shot. I just love your shoes. Have you seen how much weight Brenda lost? I bet she's having an affair." And so on.

You can't help wondering what's going on in these people's homes. Have their families stopped talking to them altogether? Are they playing tennis primarily because they have a captive audience for their commentary?

To find an explanation, I searched a few psychological websites and discovered that there is a condition known as Excessive Talking Syndrome. The causes fall into one of two categories:

1) Brain related, which includes people with ADHD, bipolar disorder and Asperger's Syndrome.

2) Non-brain related, which includes people with Histrionic Personality Disorder ("Listen to me, please.") and Narcissistic Personality Disorder ("Listen to me, I'm fabulous.")

Of course, there is another, much simpler explanation: Some people just can't shut up.

The Meshuggenehs
Meshuggeneh: A crazy person

We all know these players. They're the ones who, within 20 minutes after starting a match, begin pitching fits, throwing rackets and generally making asses of themselves.

Playing meshuggenehs is not like playing normal opponents. Against normal opponents you move the ball around with as much pace as you can control, hitting shots that are difficult for them. Against meshuggenehs you hit shots that will eventually send them into a complete meltdown. Floaters deep down the middle work well.

At first they'll put a few of them away, but since they have to swing pretty hard to generate pace, they will eventually start to miss. This will frustrate them because it seems like such an easy shot to hit. As they become increasingly frustrated, they will swing even harder and miss even more, which will eventually cause a psychotic breakdown.

Now I ask you: Is there any better feeling on a tennis court than knowing you have driven your opponent over the cliff of insanity? And is there any sweeter sound than that of a $250 racket being smashed? (As long as it's not yours, of course.)

I do have one fear about inciting a meshuggeneh. I am afraid that aliens from an advanced civilization will show up at a tennis club one Saturday just to see how humans behave in a competitive environment. They will observe a meshuggeneh throwing a full-blown tantrum and think, *This species is crazy. We'd better exterminate them before they spread throughout the universe.* Granted, it's not one of my top ten fears, but it's on the list.

The Dreaded Drop-Shotters

The drop shot, when executed properly, can be a real killer... literally. More tennis players have died running down drop shots than any other on-court maneuver. The only possible exception is the "tweener," the between-the-legs, back-to-the-net return of a deep lob. But that's more like suicide than homicide.

Playing against an expert drop-shotter can be very challenging because there's not much you can do with a ball that lands just over the high part of the net with heavy backspin and almost no bounce. Basically, you have three options.

1) You can tap the ball back lightly over the net. However, this requires a very deft touch and is extremely difficult to do when you're stretched out and on the run. Unless you hit it perfectly your opponents will get to it easily, and, since you are so close to the net, they will simply flip the ball over your head. You can either let it go and concede the point, or run like the dickens to chase it down. This will likely result in another drop shot followed by another lob, and you will soon feel like a masochistic marionette being manipulated by a sadistic puppeteer. You will not only lose the point, but you will look like a damn fool doing so.

2) You can push the ball deep into the corner. However, your opponents will be expecting this response and you'll be back in the drop shot/lob cycle, just as you were in option 1.

3) You can completely avoid the situation by refusing to play opponents who overuse the drop shot. "Overuse" is the operative word here because everyone utilizes the drop shot from time to time. It's the people who use it on virtually every point who are the problem. If we all take the approach of not playing with chronic drop-shotters, they will only be able to play each other. Eventually, most will be killed off running down drop shots and the few that remain will be so worn out they will give up the game. The world, well, the tennis world, will be a better place for it.

The Much Maligned Moonballers

If drop-shotters are the sadists of the tennis world then moonballers are the masochists. How else can you explain people adopting a style of play that requires them to…

- Be on the defensive most of the time
- Run their tails off
- Win the majority of their points by boring their opponents into a coma

In addition, moonballers are usually at the bottom of the tennis hierarchy, disdained even by dinkers and drop-shotters. It's hard to imagine that someone starting out in tennis would aspire to be a moonballer; nor is it likely that parents encourage their kids to go that route. You never hear a tennis dad say, "That's my boy, the best moonballer in the state."

It's like the guy whose son is captain of the cheerleading squad. A man just doesn't boast about that sort of thing to his poker buddies.

The cause of moonballism has been a topic of raging debate among tennis psychologists for years. Some say it is more environmental than hereditary—that being a moonballer is a conscious choice rather than a biological imperative.

However, this viewpoint raises the question as to why anyone would deliberately choose a path that brings them ridicule and ostracism.

Increasingly, psychologists are coming to accept the idea that moonballism is an inherited trait, like hair color or excessive ball-bouncing. Indeed, most moonballers say that even at a very young age they were transfixed by the sight of a high floating ball, arcing majestically across the sky, then gently landing within a few feet of the baseline, creating awkward, high-bouncing shots for their opponents.

If so, then why can't we, the non-moonballing tennis community, open our arms and our hearts to moonballers and say to them, "While your play-style might not appeal to us personally, it is, nevertheless, as valid as any other and we welcome you as our brothers and sisters under the great retractable tennis dome."

Furthermore, we should avoid passing judgment when moonballers unite to form doubles teams. Do they not have the same right to "...life, liberty and happiness" as non-moonballers? Therefore, we should not just tolerate but celebrate the union of moonballers. As incongruous as it may seem, they form partnerships that are just as close and long-lasting as those of non-moonballers.

Consequently, the time has come to cast off the archaic prejudices against moonballers and accept them as equals. In doing so we are not just being fair and open-minded, we are, in fact, acknowledging the latent moonballer in all of us.

The Countdown Servers

We all go through our little routines when we get ready to serve. We make sure our feet are in the right position, get our rackets ready, bounce the ball a time or two, then fire away.

But there are some people who carry their pre-service routines to ridiculous extremes. They always add a few extra tics, twitches and ball bounces to their routine before they are ready to serve. As the receiver, you *think* they're ready to serve when they stop all the fidgeting. But no, they just stand there. You lean forward in anticipation of the serve and think, *Okay, here it comes,* but they're completely still. Finally, you relax and, of course, that's when they decide to serve.

I often wonder what these folks are thinking as they're standing there. Are they going through some kind of checklist the way NASA does before a rocket launch, querying their various body systems a la Mission Control, such as...

Nervous system report: A-OK

Skeletal system report: Looking good

Cardiovascular system report: Functioning well

After which, Mission Control announces to the rest of the body: "All systems are go for service. Proceed with toss."

The Martians

No one knows where these people learned to play tennis, but it certainly wasn't on this planet. There isn't a single shot in their arsenal that even remotely resembles a normal stroke. They hit backhands with a forehand grip and forehands with a slasher grip. They slice, dice, hack, chop and mince the ball. It's like playing against a food processor.

There is no rhyme or reason to their game. They come in on floaters up the middle and dink serves that barely clear the net. They hit sidespin, backspin and spins that can only be described by the equations of Quantum Mechanics.

When you watch a Martian play you invariably think, *This guy is terrible. I should kill him.* But when you actually play

Some people learned the game on this dude's planet.

against one it rarely works out that way. Furthermore, you notice some unsettling aspects about their game.

1) They never allow you to get into any kind of rhythm because they never hit the same shot twice, let alone a normal shot.

2) They can get to almost any ball you hit and somehow keep it in play.

3) They can run all day.

This is because most Martians came to tennis late in their lives but were very good athletes in other sports. So they are fast, fit and very competitive.

How do you play a Martian? First off, you do *not* try and rally with them because you will soon be playing their game. By the second set you'll be contemplating "tennicide"—self-inflicted death by choking on your racket handle.

What you have to do is hit the ball way harder than you normally do and go for winners at every opportunity. Of course, you'll make a lot of errors and probably lose the match, but you'll keep the points short, thereby preserving your sanity. If you don't follow this advice then bring plenty of extra rackets to the court. You're gonna need 'em.

The Warm-up Jerks

These are the people who think the warm-up is a practice session. They hit their groundstrokes to the corners, angle off their volleys and even try a few drop-shots. When you're at the net they try to drill you with their forehands.

For the sake of civility most tennis players let them get away it, but you really shouldn't. However, your options are limited to the following:

1) Explaining to them that it's not proper tennis etiquette. That rarely works.

2) Doing the same to them. That is, going for winners and not giving them any decent warm-up shots. When they ask what you're doing, you just say, "The same thing you're doing." That sometimes works.

3) Canceling at the last minute. That always works.

The Klutzes

These are the people who are so uncoordinated you wonder how they dress themselves in the morning. Although they've been playing tennis for years, they always look as if it's their first time out.

When they're on the court their limbs appear to be acting independently of each other, with no synchronized control signals coming from their brains. Their regular teaching pros often say to them, "Please don't tell anyone you take lessons from me." If the tennis rating system used negative numbers, they'd be -4.5s.

But they're such nice people and they try so hard that everyone makes allowances for them. When you play against klutzes you actually try to hit their rackets with the ball. If by some miracle a klutz happens to hit a winner, everyone on the court, opponents and passersby included, gives them high fives. They do so very carefully, however, because they've been known to injure themselves while performing this activity.

When you see klutzes in action you know you are watching people with a true passion for the sport. And is that not the real spirit of tennis, to be out there for the love of the game no matter how badly you play?

So I say, "Here's to the klutzes. May you continue to butcher your backhands, flub your forehands and spray your serves for as long as your rubbery legs can carry you onto a tennis court."

The Squirrels

The name is taken from the expression, "Even a blind squirrel finds an acorn once in a while." The acorns for tennis squirrels are mis-hit winners, which are their most effective weapon. In fact, mis-hits are the main part of their game because when they hit the ball anywhere near the sweet spot it usually flies out. Furthermore, their mis-hits have such weird spins and land in such unexpected court locations that they are often winners. Then the squirrels apologize profusely and say, "Even a blind squirrel…"

The Well-Groomed Hackers

These are the people, usually males, who come to the court looking fabulous. They are fit, trim and togged out in the latest and most fashionable tennis attire. They have excellent form on their strokes and when you watch one of them warm up, you think, *This guy is really good.* Then the match starts and he can't hit two shots in a row. He can miss any shot from any place on the court, but he looks damn good doing so. And that's all he really cares about.

The Court Nazis

These are the ones who think they're in charge from the moment they show up at the courts. They decide who will play with whom and always pick the strongest partners for themselves. They choose the courts, the balls and even make up a few special rules in their favor. The only thing they haven't figured out is why, when they're at the net, everyone tries to drill them.

The "How far was it out?" Twits

We all ask this question on occasion but the twits do so at least a dozen times a match. After a while you want to scream, "What's the difference? Out is out! You don't get partial credit!"

Apparently, these guys think they're artillery commanders trying to zero in on a target, except that they never do. They just keep hitting the same shots out by the same margins.

In one of my regular doubles groups there was a member who was really bad about this. So another member decided to teach him a lesson by bringing a measuring tape to the court. He clipped the tape to his shorts and when the guy asked his first, "How far was it out?" question, he walked over to the ballmark, pulled out the tape, bent down and took two separate measurements.

Then he stood up and asked, "You want it in inches or centimeters?"

Without hesitation the guy said, "Both, please."

The Constant Scorekeepers

When it's their turn to serve they step up to the line and announce the complete score. "One-one, love-love, first serve." If they miss the first serve they say, "One-one, love-love, second serve."

At which point you think, *If he keeps this up I'll have to kill him before the first set is over. I just hope I get a tennis-playing judge because when I explain the circumstances he'll see it as justifiable homicide.*

The Wayward Doubles Partners

These are the players whose movement around the court bears no relation to the point being played. They move back when you're coming in, and in when you're going back. If you get pulled wide they cover their own alley, leaving a truck-sized hole up the middle. Sometimes they cut in front of you to take a shot and other times they step away from a shot that is clearly theirs. On occasion, they end up directly behind you in the I-formation.

I once had a partner like this and when I asked what exactly he was accomplishing by his crazy movements, he replied, "I'm trying to confuse our opponents."

"The only reason they look confused," I said, "is because they're laughing so hard they can hardly stand up. But you are confusing *me*. Why don't you stay in one place so I at least know where the hell you are?" It didn't work.

The "So nice it's nauseating" Ladies

These are the players, women more so than men, who are way too nice on the court. When you blow an easy shot they remark oh so sympathetically, "Good try. Such a shame you missed." And if they hit a really good one they apologize for it. "Sorry," they say, "I was just lucky." It's not just nauseating, it's downright insulting. If we get beat we get beat, we can handle it. We don't want pity.

Of course, when they're losing, the niceness act disappears very fast. They still say the same things but the inflection changes dramatically. "Such a shame you missed," comes off as, "Die, scumbag."

Saving the Worst for Last

When my birthday rolls around, my wife always asks me if there's anything special I want. I always tell her the same thing. "I want a tennis racket that has a laser death ray built into the handle." She never gets me one, claiming they are not yet available, but she probably thinks that a man who has trouble operating a cell phone shouldn't have a death ray at his disposal. However, if I ever get my hands on one, these are the players on whom I'd use it.

The Uber-Snobs

These people fancy themselves as truly superior players, in the 4.5 - 5.0 range. However, they are, at best, 3.5 - 4.0s. When they have to play with people whom they consider beneath them (but are actually at their level) they make no effort to hide their contempt. They snicker, sneer, roll their eyes and mutter insults that are not quite under their breath.

If you end up with an uber-snob as your partner the short lob is once again your best friend. Since your opponents hate them as much as you do, they will go after them every chance they get. It's not as good as the laser death ray, but it will suffice until some racket manufacturer comes out with one.

The "Win at all costs" Cheaters

Very few of us consider a tennis match to be a matter of life and death. If we play decently and lose it just means our opponents were better that day. We can live with it.

But the "win at all costs" cheaters cannot. They play for one purpose only—to win. And they will do whatever is necessary to accomplish that end, including giving bad line calls, stalling when they are losing and rushing when they are winning. They suck the enjoyment out of the game for everyone.

I asked a psychologist friend of mine, who is also a tennis player, what's up with these people. He said, "Well, some are extremely insecure and some probably had parents who were hyper-critical. Personally, I think most of 'em are just born a-holes and can't help themselves."

Player Quotes

"Whatever I said last year, just copy it. I'm sure it still fits."
Andy Roddick, after losing in the first round at the French Open

"Every generation has its own Goran. So I was the Goran of this generation."
Goran Ivanisevic

"I can't believe he is dumping me, his buddy for seven years, for a kid he's never seen before."
Paul Haarhuis, complaining about his doubles partner Jacco Eltingh flying home from the US Open for the birth of his son

"At the end I couldn't hear what the Queen was saying to me, but it was great to see her lips moving."
Virginia Wade, after winning Wimbledon

"I'm not worried about the weekend, I'm worried about Saturday."
Pete Sampras

"He told me how much he enjoyed playing me, and that he hoped it happens a lot more in the future. That makes one of us."
Andre Agassi, on being asked what Roger Federer had said to him at the net after beating him in the Australian Open

"I am the best tennis player who cannot play tennis."
Ion Tiriac

"I played a great first point."
Tim Henman after losing 6-0 6-3 to Pete Sampras

Chapter VI

The Ten Commandments of Tennis
(As copied from the tablets received on Mount Wimbledon by Moishe Wingfield)

Commandment I

I am Tennis, the Supreme Racket Sport, who brought thee out of the land of lethargy and out of the house of laziness.
Thou shalt have no other racket sports before me.

Not to disparage other fine games such as badminton, racquetball and squash, but there can be only one Supreme Racket Sport and that would be tennis. Sadly, there are many "atennists" who deny the existence of the Supreme Racket Sport. But they do so at their peril, for who among us can say why so many net cords go against them at crucial times in a match?

Commandment II

Thou shalt not make unto thee any graven image that is in the earth beneath, or that is on the court.

This is a tough one to keep because, let's be honest here, we all like trophies. And what is a trophy if not a graven image? However, some are so large and gaudy that they cannot even be displayed, much less worshiped.

I remember playing in the finals of a club mixed doubles tournament when a friend of mine rushed up to me and shouted, "Do NOT win this match! I just saw the trophy and it's big enough to melt down and make a full-sized Buick!" Fortunately, we lost.

Commandment III

Thou shalt not take the name of Tennis in vain.

Another tough one because when you blow a sitter on an important point it's pretty hard to refrain from using colorful language. However, we could all upgrade our on-court tantrums by using high-class expressions like these.

- A pox on my overhead!
- Out, out, vile volley!
- I curse thee, wretched backhand!

Commandment IV

Remember thy Tennis date to keep it holy.

Far too many people treat their tennis dates as just another day. They cancel on a whim or use flimsy excuses such as, "I didn't get much sleep last night." Or, "My wife is having a baby."

This is unacceptable behavior; one might even call it blasphemy. Tennis matches are sacred events, like Super Bowls and Bar Mitzvahs.

By canceling tennis dates you not only disappoint your partners but you dishonor the memory of the pioneers who blazed the way for you. Also, you'll get a reputation for being a "tennis tease" and no one will play with you anymore.

Commandment V

Honor thy let cords and thy luck shots.

This is an easy one to keep because when you win a point with a lucky shot, all it takes is a wave of the racket as if to say, "I am *so* sorry I won a point that way, even though I'm really not, just as you wouldn't be, but we all have to go through this silly charade because the culture of the sport demands it."

Commandment VI

Thou shalt kill thy opponents' short lobs.

However, thou shalt not try and kill thy opponents. Aim it at their feet or at the open court. Do not go head-hunting with an easy overhead. If you do so regularly, people will go after you. Furthermore, the tennis gods will start pulling the trigger on your hamstrings.

Commandment VII

Thou shalt not commit gamesmanship.

This is a gray area but we all know when we've crossed the line. For example, if your opponent mangles an easy overhead and shouts, "That's the worst overhead I've ever hit!" Don't say, "I've seen you hit worse ones than that."

Also, don't offer nonsensical advice such as, "Hope you don't mind my saying this, but your left hip is misaligned with the axis of your core. Try to keep it in line better."

Finally, if your opponent who normally has a shaky serve is hitting it extremely well, do not say, "You're really serving great today. You haven't double-faulted once... yet." Seriously, you should never, ever say things like that. (Unless you really need to.)

Commandment VIII

Thou shalt not steal thy opponents' glory when thou lose.

If you lose a match, especially to someone you think you should beat, do not shake hands and say, "That's the worst match I've ever played. I shouldn't lose to you even if I had a sucking chest wound." It's very ungracious.

What you say is, "Good match, you played well." Yes, it's painful and yes, you'd rather chew glass, or, better yet, wrap your racket around your opponent's head, but you can't. You have to be a good sport and you have to keep saying to yourself, "It's just a tennis match; it's not that important." (That doesn't work for me either, but it seems like the right thing to say.)

Commandment IX

Thou shalt not bear false witness on line calls.

You're serving down set point and your opponent hits a passing shot that lands extremely close to the line. You are 99.9% sure the ball was out. What's your call?

If you answered "good" then good for you and you can skip to the next commandment. If you answered "out" or are lying about calling it in, please continue.

A) You know you're supposed to call it in unless you're 100% sure it's out, right? (Yes/No)

B) If you win the match on a bad line call you're going to feel badly about it later on, right? (Yes/No)

C) If your opponent is giving bad line calls you can do the same, right? (Yes/No)

Answer key: A) Yes; B) Yes; C) Yes or No, depending on the size of your opponent.

Unless you're in a tournament where you can call for an umpire, playing against a cheater puts the honest competitor in a very difficult position. In general, your choices are limited to walking off the court, playing through it, giving your opponent bad calls or pulling out the laser death ray in your racket handle. (You wish.)

Commandment X

Thou shalt not covet thy neighbor's strokes.

No matter what your level of play, there are always people in your group with better strokes. You can't help being covetous and often think, *If I just had her backhand,* or, *If I only had his serve.* Well, you don't. Your game is your game and if you've been playing for a good many years you've reached a plateau.

Furthermore, coveting other people's games is not going to help you. However, if you give it your all every time you go out there, if you always play fairly and honestly, the ones with superior strokes might just be covetous of you. Unfortunately, they'll still kick your tail.

Commentator Quotes

"Tim Henman, I guess, is sitting in the locker room, pacing up and down."
John Inverdale

"When Martina is tense it helps her relax."
Dan Maskel

"Billie Jean King, with the look on her face that says she can't believe it, because she never believes it, and yet, somehow, I think she does."
Max Robertson

"That's one of the best sets I've seen him play, although I should preface that by saying I haven't seen him play before."
John McEnroe

"Let's hope he can force him into those unforced errors."
Tim Henman

"Even when he has to move back, he moves back so that he's moving forwards."
Mark Cox

"Ann's got to take her nerve by the horns."
Virginia Wade

"Diane is keeping her head beautifully on her shoulders."
Ann Jones

"Chip Hooper is such a big man that it is sometimes difficult to see where he is on the court."
Mark Cox

Chapter VII

The Senior Game
(It Was the Best of Tennis,
It Was the Worst of Tennis)

I was watching a doubles match between a couple of pretty good senior teams, and marveling at how long most of the points were lasting. I asked the guy next to me, who was also watching, "Is this the best of senior tennis because they keep the ball in play so well or is it the worst of senior tennis because no one can put it away?"

His response was Zen-like. "There's really no difference," he said. "At a high level of senior tennis there is no 'A' game or 'C' game," just a solid 'B' game. They never play badly, they never play great, they just play really well all the time."

Then I asked the guy, who seemed very wise on the subject, "How do you know when you are ready for senior tennis?" He thought about it for a few seconds and said, "Let me get back to you." The next day he handed me this list.

You know you're ready for senior tennis when…

- You can beat your second serve to the net.

- A mis-hit volley is your best offensive weapon.

- You use the lob as an approach shot.

- You hit drop shot overheads on purpose.

- You can remember when a two-handed backhand was a rarity.

- You start losing to your grandchildren.

- You spend more time talking about your injuries than your tennis game.

- You know how to measure the net height with a wood racket.

- You've mastered the lob-volley.

- You wear a warm-up jacket when the temperature drops below 72 degrees.

- You remember carrying a first-aid kit to the courts in case you lacerated yourself opening a can of balls.

There are a couple of points to be made about the list. The first is that the lob figures in pretty heavily, which is not surprising since it's the go-to shot for seniors. The second is that the list applies to average or even above-average seniors, not to the top-level ones. These folks are fast, fit and can hit with plenty of pace and uncanny control. You might picture a 73-year-old tennis player as someone with creaky knees and arthritic hips who can barely get around the court, but if you were to watch a couple of top-rated seniors go at it, you would quickly be disabused of that notion.

Here's a piece of advice: Unless your rating is 4.5 or above, do not play a highly ranked senior. You will be jerked around unmercifully. The only time you'll spend in the middle of the court is when you're streaking across it to get to the other side. After you finish the match you'll feel like a load of laundry—tumbled, rinsed, spun and hung out to dry.

Advancing to the realm of senior tennis causes genuine concern among many people because they feel it's a major milestone in the march to old age. But it really shouldn't trouble anyone. As the old adage says: "You don't stop moving because you get old, you get old because you stop moving." Well, it sounds nice anyway.

The Senior Skill Set

By the time you join the senior ranks you will find that your skills and athleticism have declined a bit. This should not concern you because you will develop new skills to compensate for it, some of which are needed for basic survival in the senior ranks. Here are a few examples.

The timely "yours!"

One such skill is the ability to yell "yours!" on a timely basis. This may seem like a trivial matter but if you have doubles partners who are good at this you'll be chasing down all the deep lobs. This gets very old very fast.

To develop this skill you have to practice it, just like any other skill. Here's what you do: Have your spouse, or, better yet, someone who doesn't think you should be institutionalized, toss balls at you while you're in the ready position. They should vary the trajectory of the toss just as it would vary in a match. The idea is that as soon as you see a ball that will go over your head, you immediately and automatically yell "yours!"

Once you've perfected this skill you're ready for senior doubles. From then on, all you have to do is tell your partners what a great job they're doing running down all those lobs. Just make sure you have plenty of replacement partners.

The art of the excuse

Another skill you have to master is how to utilize "pre-emptive excuses" or simply "precuses." Precuses are basically excuses you use *before* a match to explain why you are not going to play well. The two categories of precuses are medical and conditional.

Medical precuses include all the ailments you currently have plus any you've incurred in the past ten years that could, in any way, affect your strokes and movement. Accomplished senior players bring along detailed medical histories including MRI scans, blood tests and physician's notes to back up their claims.

Conditional precuses are a bit more contrived and include statements such as, "I just can't volley if the atmospheric pressure is less than 29.92 inches of mercury." And, "This phase of the lunar cycle really screws up my backhand." Everyone knows it's a load of bull, but they'll still admire you for your creativity.

Advanced pikery

The final skill you acquire as a senior, and this one is optional, is frugality. If like many seniors you're on a tight budget or like others you're just a cheapskate, you'll want to stretch your tennis dollar as far as possible. Since you have to have a decent racket, strings and footwear, there's not much to save there. That leaves attire and balls.

As for attire, a lot of seniors are wearing the same outfits they wore during the Carter administration. Their clothes appear to be one wash cycle away from disintegration but somehow they're hanging on by a thread... almost literally. They just have to keep them away from their wives who would cheerfully toss them out, even if they were being worn at the time.

Although tennis balls haven't increased in price for many years, they still represent a significant expense—unless you never open a new can, something you rarely have to do if you're always the last one to show up for a match. One legendary piker was so adept at this practice, and carried the same can of balls around for so long, that when he finally cracked it open he had to roll a thin piece of metal around the top to get the lid off. The balls, of course, were white.

Senior Benefits

In addition to the above, there are some real benefits to joining the senior ranks. The best ones are...

Medical benefits

Playing senior tennis is like going to medical school for free. Med students pay hundreds of thousands of dollars to get the kind of education one can acquire just by listening to a group of senior players chat for a while. This is particularly true in the field of orthopedics. By the time tennis players reach the age of 65, they have strained, sprained, torn and hyper-extended most of the tendons, ligaments and muscles in their bodies, and they know the causes, symptoms and treatments for each.

In fact, seniors are so good at describing their injuries that the conversation often sounds like a poker game. For example, one guy will open with a torn meniscus and another guy will immediately say, "Is that all you got? I can beat you easily with a pair of ruptured discs." Then a third guy will pull up his shirt and say, "Sorry, gents, read 'em and weep, four-of-a-kind arterial bypasses."

He looks like a winner until the guy with a prostate full of radioactive implants antes up and nukes everyone. (A friend of mine was going through this procedure and I asked him if there were any serious side effects. "Actually," he said, "the biggest side effect has been a positive one. When I go to the bathroom in the middle of the night I don't have to turn the light on.")

Score-keeping fun

The other advantage to the senior game is that you can have a lot of fun with the score. For example, say you're serving at 15-40 and just for kicks you announce the score as 30-all. At least one person on the other team will challenge you on it, so you say, "Let's review the points." That's when the fun begins because the ensuing conversation goes something like this:

"Didn't I hit a backhand winner on the first point?" says the first guy.

Seniors in a spirited game of competitive injuries.

Whereupon the next guy says, "You? Hell no, that was me."

Then another says, "I remember hitting an overhead that you guys couldn't touch."

Yet another says, "That's because you shanked it into a tree."

And so on. After enjoying this exercise in short-term memory loss for a while you finally say, "I was wrong. It's 15-40." After all, you just want to have some fun, you don't want to cheat.

Senior Records

Although not as well-known as the records for professionals, the records for senior players are, in their own way, every bit as impressive. They include the following:

- Most lobs in a single point: 11
- Most drop-shots in a single point: 6
- Most braces worn in a match: 7 (2 knee, 2 ankle, 1 wrist, 1 shoulder and 1 elbow)
  A special mention goes to a guy I saw playing in a full neck brace. Initially, I thought he was crazy, but I later decided he was a true tennis hero for risking permanent paralysis rather than forgo a single day of playing.
- Most painkiller brands in a tennis bag:
  Over the counter: 4
  Prescription: 3
- Most artificial joints (combined):
  Singles: 4
  Doubles: 7
- Largest quantity of ibuprofen ingested before a match:
  Individual: 1600 milligrams
  Doubles team: 2400 milligrams
- Most time spent arguing over a line call: 7 minutes

- Most times losing track of the score in one game: 5
- Most bathroom breaks in a three-set match (combined):
  Singles: 5
  Doubles: 8
- Most time spent debating doubles strategy between points: 2.5 minutes
- Longest three-set match: 5.5 hours (2 hours of playing; 3.5 hours of schmoozing)

In conclusion, you shouldn't be at all concerned about becoming a senior tennis player if for no other reason than it means you're still alive. (There is a negative corollary to this idea. If, as a senior player, you wake up in the morning and nothing hurts, it means you're dead.)

Player Quotes

"I still break racquets, but now I do it in a positive way."
Goran Ivanisevic

"About 11 Grand Slams."
Pete Sampras, on being asked to pinpoint the difference between himself and Pat Rafter

"I started when I was four, but I didn't play seriously until I was eight."
Kathy Rinaldi

"Nobody's perfect... except Roger."
Marat Safin, commenting on Roger Federer's year in 2006

"She [Serena Williams] played some great shots, but so did I, and that was the only difference."
Jennifer Capriati

"A win's a win, unless it is not a win, and then it's not a win."
Venus Williams

"New Yorkers love it when you spill your guts. At Wimbledon they make you clean it up."
Jimmy Connors

"My serve has killed a small dog... I'm joking, I'm joking! The dog was huge!"
Andy Roddick

"I hate this game."
At least once in their lives, pretty much everyone who has played serious tennis

Chapter VIII

A Brief History of the Game

PART I

According to the latest ideas in theoretical physics, the universe was not created by a fortuitous sequence of random events. Rather, it was purposefully designed so that the dominant species on a habitable planet would engage in striking a spherical projectile while uttering self-deprecating obscenities. This concept is known as the Big Backhand Theory.

Prehistory

Whatever the reason for the universe, we do know that tennis history goes back a long way (but then, pretty much all of history goes back a long way.) In fact, newly uncovered fossil remains indicate that a bipedal human ancestor named *homo hackus* may have died from a spinal injury sustained while trying to hit a bouncing overhead.

The Greeks

Many tennis historians believe that the basic idea of the game originated in ancient Greece. A heretofore unknown translation of Plato's *Dialogues* reveals the following: Plato and his student, Aristotle, are out for a walk while pondering the nature of existence. Suddenly, and for no apparent reason, Aristotle picks up an acorn and swats it over to Plato.

"Hey P-man," Aristotle shouts, "acorn comin' at ya. Smack it back!"

To which Plato replies, "Yes, I see it, but I would ask this: Is the acorn moving towards me or am I moving towards the acorn? It's quite the conundrum."

"Dude, you are such a twit," says Aristotle.

As can be surmised, the game didn't get very far in Greece.

The Romans

There are also references to tennis during the glory days of the Roman Empire. However, the citizens of Rome, as is true of Italians today, could never agree on a standard set of rules. In the two years that a tennis-like game was played in the empire, there were four different governing bodies each with its own unique code of regulations. In addition, there were seven high commissioners who spent most of their time hitting on teenage ball girls. The current Italian government is based on this model, except that it is even more disorganized.

The Barbarians

There was a brief renewal of interest in tennis after the barbarians sacked Rome, but it didn't become popular as it was too much of a head game—primarily because they used actual heads. Tennis was again tried in the Dark Ages but with such poor lighting it was impossible to play a decent match. And don't even talk about the line calls.

The French

A tennis-like game became popular in Europe among medieval monks, who, being celibate, were pretty desperate for a physical outlet. It caught on in the French Royal Court where it was played by hitting a leather ball back and forth with the hand. It was called "jeu de paumme," literally "game of the palm" (not to be confused with another "game of the palm" that is popular among males, both tennis players as well as non- tennis players).

The French called their game "tenez," which literally means, "You CANNOT be serious!" Ha ha. No, it just means "take it," indicating that the ball was about to be served (although you'd think people could have figured that out for themselves).

Tennis Scoring Digression

Before continuing with the history of tennis, a few words about tennis scoring, which is surely the most bizarre of all major sports, are in order. If you search the web for the story behind tennis scoring you find a variety of theories and references, from quarter-hour clock times, to court positions, to British naval guns. However, since the game originated in France, and the French are known for messing with people's heads, the following should be included among the various theories.

A couple of French women, Monique and Simone, who are on the tenez rules committee, are in a bar sipping wine when Monique says to Simone, "You know something, Simone?"

"I know many things," says Simone, "For example, I know that…"

(Monique whacks her in the head.)

"Silence! It wasn't a question, it was a lead-in," says Monique.

"Oww, sorry. Lead-in to what?" asks Simone.

"I was going to say that we should create a nonsensical scoring system for our game," responds Monique.

"Why would we do that?" asks Simone.

"To screw with people's heads," says Monique.

"But why?"

"Because we are French. It's what we do."

"Right, I forgot. So what did you have in mind?"

"Well, take the first point. Instead of calling it 'one' we could call it, oh I don't know, 'fifteen.'"

"Why 'fifteen?'"

"No reason. I just like it."

"Okay. So the second point would be 'thirty?'"

"Right."

"And the third point 'forty-five?'"

"No. It would be 'forty.'"

"'Forty?' But that makes no sense."

"Exactly."

"Would the fourth point be 'fifty?'"

"No, it would have no value. It would just be the end of the game."

"So you win the game with a point that has no value?"

"Right."

"That will drive people crazy. I love it!"

"Speaking of love…"

PART II

Sport of kings

Louis X, who was king of France in the early 1300s, was an avid tennis player but wasn't too keen on playing outdoors, so he had indoor courts constructed. That's the best part about being a tennis-playing king. If you don't like the courts or conditions, you have your people build ones you do like. The indoor game, which included hitting the ball off a wall, has been dubbed "Royal (or Real) Tennis."

Befitting of royal privilege, Louis had an amazing won/loss record, as did all the monarchs who took up the game. People who went around bragging that they beat the king needed to have their heads examined, usually during the autopsy.

Louis died in 1316 after a particularly strenuous tennis match followed by a bout of prodigious drinking. However, some historians suspect that he was poisoned as a result of a heated debate over an egregious line call.

Tennis continued as a hand sport for another 500 years until a couple of guys in England decided to use rackets. Their names were Harry Gem and Augurio Perera, and in 1872 they opened the first outdoor tennis club in England.

Enter the major

The man who is credited with creating and popularizing the modern game (circa 1874) is a British army officer named Major Walter Clopton Wingfield. That was the good part. The bad part was that he called the sport by the most inelegant name of "sphairistike." The word is from the ancient Greek and is loosely translated as, "a game with balls." (I swear; you can look it up.)

Wingfield discovered his mistake when he tried to recruit ladies to the sport. Oftentimes, he would approach a woman and say, "Excuse me, madam, would you like to engage in sphairistike with me? I could teach you how to do it."

After getting thrashed a few times, Wingfield realized his error and changed the name to "Lawn Tennis." He was heavily involved in establishing the basic rules of the game, many of which are still in use today. To round out his story, Wingfield endured terrible personal tragedies when three of his sons died young and his wife suffered severe mental illness. After that he lost his passion for tennis but developed an interest in the culinary arts. He even founded a gourmet cooking society named "Le Cordon Rouge." You really have to admire a guy whose primary pursuits in life are food and tennis. Wingfield was inducted into the International Tennis Hall of Fame in 1997.

The Brits take over

The focal point of tennis shifted from France to England, particularly when, in the spring of 1877, "The All England

Croquet and Lawn Tennis Club" instituted the first Lawn Tennis tournament. Eventually, the tournament came to be known as simply, "The Championships."

The club officers created many of their own rules for running the tournament. One rule, exemplifying British snootiness, stated that, "Play shall begin at 2:00 PM *precisely* on the first Monday of the fortnight." The implication being, "If play does not start at this time, all of England, nay the entire British Empire, will collapse like a mortally wounded animal, whereupon ignorant savages who cannot even start a tennis tournament on time will feed on its rotting carcass." Okay, that last part was a melodramatic embellishment, but the British can be pretty snooty about their rules.

Tennis comes to America

The person who is credited with bringing tennis to the United States is Mary Ewing Outerbridge of Staten Island, New York. Miss Outerbridge was vacationing in Bermuda in 1874 and witnessed a lawn tennis match played by British military officers. Intrigued, she talked them into letting her give the game a try. The experience for Mary, as is true for millions of us, was love at first strike. She brought back a rule book, a net, balls and rackets, and set up the first tennis court at the Staten Island Cricket & Baseball Club.

In addition to having the first tennis court in America, Staten Island is also famous for:

1) The Staten Island ferry that runs between Manhattan and the island. *(Bet you knew that.)*

2) The Staten Island Zoo, which maintains the most complete rattlesnake collection in the world with 39 varieties. *(Bet you didn't know that.)*

3) The nation's largest landfill. (At one time, anyway.) *(Bet you didn't want to know that.)*

It is fitting that a woman played an important role in tennis history because women have been well-represented in the sport from its very beginning—although not on an equal basis with men until the major tournaments began awarding comparable prize money. On a side note, I remember a couple of local radio sports talk guys discussing the equal pay status of women when one of them remarked, "Tennis is truly a bisexual sport." The other guy was laughing so hard he had to go off mike.

A worldwide sport

During the late 1800s and early 1900s tennis spread throughout the world primarily because the Brits, who were in the throes of empire building, schlepped along all things British wherever they went.

By the early twentieth century the four major tournaments were in operation including Wimbledon in 1877, the US Open in 1881, the French Open in 1891 and the Australian Open in 1905. In addition, Dwight Davis, an accomplished tennis player and lawyer, began a men's competition between the US and England that eventually became an international event known, not surprisingly, as the Davis Cup.

For many years, winning the Davis Cup was arguably the most prestigious accomplishment in international tennis. However, like the Miss America pageant, the Davis Cup has lost much of its luster and popularity. It has been suggested that having the competitors wear racier outfits would pique the publics' interest… the Miss America contestants, that is. Male tennis players in Speedos, even young, fit guys, is not a good look, especially when they're in the service return stance.

For a time, tennis shorts had become alarmingly brief.

Tennis Fashion Digression

Lawn tennis began as a genteel game played primarily by the elite, with men in full length trousers and women in long flowing dresses. Men began wearing shorts in the 1930s, and if you look at some of the photos from that time period the shorts were of a pretty reasonable length. Unfortunately, men's tennis shorts took a turn for the worse and began getting shorter and tighter until, by the 1960s, they were so restrictive that an entire generation of male tennis players was losing the ability to procreate.

In addition, they weren't the most manly looking apparel. I remember a tennis buddy of mine, who grew up in a pretty tough neighborhood in Brooklyn, telling me that he wouldn't dare go out in his little white shorts without wearing sweatpants over them. When I asked him why he answered, "In my neighborhood 'throwing someone under the bus' isn't just a figure of speech."

By the 1990s men's shorts were becoming longer and looser, which was providential because the game was becoming exponentially faster and more intense. If men had to play today's high-speed game in yesterday's "tightie whities," well, let's just say that grunting would be at a much higher pitch.

Women's tennis attire has spanned the gamut of styles including…

The ridiculous
Ladies wearing ground-scraping skirts with bustles, corsets, high necklines and floppy hats (late 1800s).

The cheeky
Suzanne Lenglen winning Wimbledon in a knee-length dress with three-quarter sleeves and a broad headband (1919).

The practical
Helen Wills Moody wearing a sleeveless white blouse and pleated skirt (1920s).

The utilitarian
Helen Jacobs donning Bermuda shorts at Forest Hills (1933).

The scandalous
Gussy Moran playing Wimbledon wearing lace-trimmed panties beneath her skirt. Photographers would lie flat on the ground to shoot her knickers. (1949).

The sublime
Anne White entering Wimbledon in a body-hugging white unitard, distracting her opponents and male members of the royal family (1985).

And back to the ridiculous
US Open champ Serena Williams playing in a shiny, skintight black bodysuit, the infamous "catsuit." (2002).

PART III

Through the early part of the twentieth century tennis gradually increased in popularity and participation. As it did so, top-flight athletes such as Bill Tilden and Suzanne Lenglen were dominating the sport. A French quartet known as the Four Horsemen were also highly competitive during that era. The quartet included Jean Borotra, Henri Cochet, René Lacoste and Jacques Brugnon.

Le Crocodile (Or Le Alligator)

The Four Horsemen were an interesting bunch, but by far the most accomplished and well-known was Lacoste. As a player, Lacoste's nickname was "Le Crocodile" so when he founded a clothing company he used an image of a crocodile as the logo. No doubt, some marketing genius said to Lacoste, "René, bubby, you play a nice game of tennis; I'll give you that. But as a businessman you're clueless. Nobody, I mean nobody, is going to buy a shirt with a flesh-eating reptile on it."

Lacoste, who was more a man of action than words, probably responded with something like, "We shall see." What we see is that Lacoste has become one of the most successful sportswear companies in the world and its reptilian logo among the most famous.

(Many people mistakenly believe the Lacoste logo depicts an alligator, which is not unreasonable because alligators and crocodiles, like dolphins and porpoises, appear to be the same creatures but with different names.)

In addition to being a champion tennis player and successful businessman, Lacoste was also an inventor. In 1963 he patented a revolutionary tubular steel racket, which was marketed in the US as the T-2000 by Wilson Sporting Goods. Wilson persuaded Jimmy Connors to use the racket and for several years in the mid 1970's, Connors ruled men's tennis.

Consequently, a horde of club players, this writer included, purchased T-2000s with the expectation of playing like Jimmy. We quickly discovered that the racket had the sweet spot of a spatula and the feel of a tire iron.

Money talks

As the popularity of tennis grew, a few top players and promoters came up with the radical idea of making some money off the sport. This idea was appalling to officials of the International Tennis Federation (ITF), which sanctions Grand Slam tournaments, so they issued the following edict: "Any individual who would be so crass as to accept money for playing competitive tennis, especially for such shallow reasons as buying food and paying rent, is hereby banned from all Grand Slam tournaments." (Or something to that effect.) The ban lasted until 1968 when the so-called Open Era began.

Nevertheless, the lure of lucre was strong and many of the top players succumbed to it. A number of pro tours with various formats were organized, but the first commercially successful one (for the men anyway) was started by Jack Kramer.

The Rocket age

One top man who resisted turning pro, initially at least, was Rod Laver. Laver had his sights set on winning major tournaments and in 1962 he won them all, completing a calendar Grand Slam.

Apparently, not everyone was impressed because somebody must have said to Laver, "Y'know, Rod, it isn't that big a deal. The world's best players weren't even in the tournaments." So in 1969, when the big guns had returned to the majors, Laver completed a second Grand Slam. This time everyone was impressed.

As the only man to win two Grand Slams, Laver has left an indelible legacy on the sport. However, his most lasting influence on the popularity of tennis may have come from a match that he lost. The occasion was the 1972 finals of the World Championship Tennis (WCT) tour. Laver's opponent was Ken (Muscles) Rosewall and they played for the then staggering sum of $50,000 which was put up by the tour's founder, Lamar (Richdude) Hunt. With that amount of money on the line and a very effective publicity campaign, more than 20 million people in the US tuned in, making it the most watched tennis broadcast up to that time.

(Note: The largest American TV audience to ever watch a tennis match—tennis farce, actually—was on September 20,

1973 when over 50 million viewers saw the over-hyped "Battle of the Sexes." The match was between a tennis champion, 29-year-old Billie Jean King, and a tennis has-been, 55-year-old Bobby Riggs, with commentary by a tennis know-nothing, Howard Cosell. It wasn't much of a match and King won easily, but it was grand theater and, arguably, Riggs' greatest hustle. For Bobby, it couldn't get any better.)

Back to Rosewall and Laver. The millions who watched their match were treated to a classic five-setter with Rosewall prevailing, but the real winner was the game itself. People saw two normal-sized guys who were terrific athletes playing a physically demanding game that requires speed, stamina and agility as well as the skill to hit a fast-moving ball while they were moving. The match is credited, at least partially, with kick-starting the tennis boom in America.

Enter the ladies

On the distaff side of the tennis family, women also saw the opportunity to make money and on several occasions approached the men to see if they were interested in joining forces. The men were not, feeling they really didn't need the women to be successful. As it turned out, the women didn't need the men either, since they could draw crowds and get decent TV ratings on their own.

In addition, once the Open Era began and the big tournaments started awarding prize money, there was a huge disparity between the paychecks of the men and women. So in 1970 the women decided to start their own professional circuit with Gladys Heldman, publisher of *World Tennis Magazine,* as the founder.

What they did need was a sponsor with deep pockets, but the only one that stepped up was the Philip Morris Company with their product Virginia Slims™ cigarettes. Virginia Slims was marketed to women with the catchy slogan, "You've come a long way, baby!" Unstated is the rest of the slogan, "You now have the same opportunity as men to get cancer, emphysema, heart disease and a host of other afflictions associated with cigarette smoking. Way to go, baby!"

It is rather ironic that a sport with such healthful benefits would promote such an unhealthy product as cigarettes, and the women took a lot of heat over it. But as one top pro explained, "If you're in a raging sea about to drown and someone throws you a lifeline, you grab it and let them pull you on board. When you discover that you've been rescued by pirates you say, 'Thank you very much,' and get the hell off the ship as soon as you can."

Eventually, the women did get off the cigarette boat and, in 1973, the Virginia Slims circuit morphed in to the Women's Tennis Association (WTA). Since then the WTA has partnered with a variety of non-carcinogenic sponsors and signed lucrative TV contracts. Today, women tennis stars are international celebrities, just as well-known as the men, and they can earn just as much money. It's doubtful you can say that about any other sport.

So ends this brief sojourn through tennis history. There are a number of excellent books that go into far greater detail and introduce many more of the characters that make up the story—the heroes and the villains, the victors and the vanquished, the saviors and the stinkers. In other words, very much like life but with better athletes in skimpier clothing.

Commentator Quotes

"These ball boys are marvelous. You don't even notice them. There's a left-handed one over there. I noticed him earlier."
Max Robertson

"The pace of this match is really accelerating, by which I mean it's getting faster all the time."
David Coleman

"You'd have to think that if he'd been around today, Rod Laver would have been Rod Laver."
Jim Courier

"Henman and Coria have met three times in the past and they've won one apiece."
Annabel Croft

"First thing is, it's inevitable. The second thing is, it's going to happen anyway."
Gerald Williams, on the dangers of building up Andy Murray

"Becker had to play every day of the second week - eight days in a row."
BBC during the Wimbledon Championships

"If she gets the jitters now, then she isn't the great champion that she is."
Max Robertson

"I had a feeling today that Venus Williams would either win or lose."
Martina Navratilova

Chapter IX

The Last Shot

For about five years I had a regular tennis partner who was a philosophy professor at a small college. We usually had very competitive matches, along with numerous engrossing discussions, although a few of them left me a bit uneasy. For some perverse reason, philosophy majors take great joy in convincing you that your most deeply held beliefs rest more on shifting sands than solid rock. (Then again, why else would someone major in philosophy?)

Still, he was a pretty good player but he had one serious flaw in his game. He would set up a point to get an easy putaway then, more often than not, miss the shot. Following one particular match in which he did this about ten times, he lamented, "Y'know something, I always miss the last shot and it really bothers me."

I thought about this for a few seconds and replied, "I think you have it backwards. You don't miss it because it's the last shot; it's the last shot because you miss it."

"Ostensibly, that's true," he said. "But I think it goes deeper than that."

"How so?" I asked, feeling myself getting pulled into a rhetorical black hole.

"Actually," he responded, "I was thinking more about the long-term, existential last shot than the immediate one."

At this point I should have said, "That's very interesting but I really have to go now." However, by this time I was inside the event horizon and unable to escape, so I said, "I'm not sure what you mean."

"Well," he began, "we all have a limited number of shots we will hit in our lives. The better, fitter players will hit more than most, but it's still a finite number. Among those shots will be a series of last shots—the last shot of a point, of a game, of a match and, eventually, the last shot of our lives. You could call it the last, last shot. As tennis players, the best we can hope for is that it's a good one."

Thus ended the conversation, so we picked up our tennis bags and trudged back to our cars. As I drove home I started thinking about the idea of the last, last shot, which is normally the sort of thing I try *not* to think about. However, in this case it had special meaning because of what happened to a close friend of mine, let's call him Dan, a few weeks earlier.

Here's the recap: It was a typical mid-August day in central Florida—sweltering heat, drenching humidity, and not even a whisper of a breeze for relief. It was a day that would give pause to even the most avid tennis player and Dan was anything but avid. He'd been feeling poorly all week and felt particularly bad on that Saturday morning. He had almost no energy and, at times, he was dizzy and short of breath—symptoms that he later wished he'd paid more attention to.

He really wanted to cancel but knew it was too late to get a sub so he got into his car and drove to the courts. From the warm-up to the final point he felt increasingly lousy and played even worse. As it happened, he was serving at match point down and double-faulted. "A miserable end to a miserable day," he thought.

Then he said his good-byes and drove back home. As soon as he walked in his house he flopped down on the couch, exhausted. Within seconds he was slammed with the crushing chest pain of a massive heart attack.

Fortunately, his wife was home so she immediately gave him a couple of aspirin tablets and called 911. A few minutes later the EMTs arrived and performed their on-the-spot magic to get him stabilized, a duty at which they have vast experience in view of Florida's aged population. They sped off in the ambulance and arrived at the hospital with the medical emergency team waiting. They rushed him into surgery, found the standard occluded cardiac arteries and performed the standard quadruple bypass procedure.

(Side note: Ever the comedian, Dan later asked the surgeon if the hospital was running a cardiac special that week, such as, buy three bypasses and get the fourth one free.)

He got out of ICU a few days later and I went to visit him in the hospital. It's always unsettling to see someone who's recently undergone a major medical event, especially if it's one of your contemporaries. He was pale and haggard and looked like he'd aged five years in the six days since his heart attack. He had the requisite IV and breathing tubes attached, along with the sensors and monitors that reduce a person's life to rhythmic beeps, blinking lights and squiggles on a screen.

We chatted for a few minutes about mundane matters and the conversation eventually drifted to his traumatic experience. I asked him if he was aware of what was going on as he was being taken to the hospital. "Very much so," he replied.

Then I asked, "What was going through your mind as they were frantically wheeling you into surgery?"

"I was thinking about my family and whether I would ever see them again," he replied. "But I was also recalling that the last thing I did on a tennis court was miss a second serve on match point, and I did not want to die with an unredeemed double fault on my soul."

He later told me that getting back on a tennis court was a definite motivating factor in his recovery. He came back well

DAN HARWICK
1945 – 2010

HERE LIES DAN
FOREVER VAULTED
ON HIS FINAL SWINGS
HE DOUBLE FAULTED

enough to play again but passed away from an unrelated illness some fifteen years later. I don't know what his last shot was, but I hope it was good.

Now I have reached an age when I can foresee that final "Out" call that awaits us all. So when I finish a match in which I've missed my last shot, I always ask the other players if anyone wants to hit for a few minutes. If no one is interested then I hit some serves. Either way, I don't pack it in until I've smacked a good one. 'Cause you never know.

Random Quotes

"It took me seventeen years to get three thousand hits in baseball. I did it in one afternoon on the golf course."
Hank Aaron

"When someone bought the second car."
Richard Petty, on being asked when auto racing began

"Dogs have masters, cats have staff."
The woman at the pet store

"Every parent wants to think their child could grow up to be president. No parent wants their child to be a politician."
John F. Kennedy

"Holding on to anger is like drinking poison and expecting your enemy to die."
Ancient proverb

"Women marry men hoping they will change and they don't. Men marry women hoping they won't change and they do."
Albert Einstein (really)

"My grandmother started walking five miles a day when she was 60. She's 97 today and we don't know where the hell she is."
Ellen DeGeneres

And finally…
"Don't watch the balls."
Sign on a tennis court fence at a nudist colony